THE VICTORIA & ALBERT MUSEUM'S TEXTILE COLLECTION

DESIGN FOR PRINTED TEXTILES IN ENGLAND FROM 1750 TO 1850

a flower'd Calicoe long sack 1746

a Blue damask Coat 1746
half a Guinea a yard

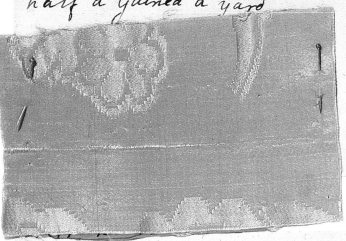

a flower'd Cotten Jacket 1747

a blue & white linnen long sack
1748

a flower'd silk Robe-Coat 1748

a Green Cambler Coat 1749

THE VICTORIA & ALBERT MUSEUM'S TEXTILE COLLECTION

DESIGN FOR PRINTED TEXTILES IN ENGLAND FROM 1750 TO 1850

BY WENDY HEFFORD

CANOPY BOOKS
A division of Abbeville Press, Inc.
NEW YORK

First published in the United States of America, 1992,
by Canopy Books, a division of Abbeville Press, Inc.,
488 Madison Avenue, New York, NY 10022.

First published in Great Britain, 1992, by the
Victoria & Albert Museum, Cromwell Road, London SW7.

Designed by Area, London

ISBN 1 55859 435 3

FRONT AND BACK COVERS:
Furnishing chintz. Probably printed at Bannister Hall, 1805-10. Circ.496-1956

FRONTISPIECE
1. Block-printed dress materials from the scrapbook made by Barbara Johnson
dating from 1746 to 1828. T.219-1973

Contents

6 ACKNOWLEDGEMENTS

Thanks are extended to Mr Donald King, the former Keeper of the Textiles Department and editor of the original edition of the three volumes *British Textile Design in the Victoria and Albert Museum* and to Mr Takahiko Sano who performed amazing feats as photographer, editorial advisor and translator of the first series. Publications are dependent upon team efforts and many curators, past and present, of the Textiles and Dress Collection helped in the preparation of these books. That they are now re-issued for a wider audience is due to the thoughtfulness of the publishers Gakken, Tokyo; the support of Jennifer Blain and Lesley Burton of V&A Publishing and the diligence of Clare Woodthorpe Browne of Textiles and Dress.

DESIGN FOR PRINTED TEXTILES IN ENGLAND 1750 TO 1850

WENDY HEFFORD

INTRODUCTION

The following text was first published in 1980, by Gakken Co. Ltd. of Tokyo, in the second volume of "British Textile Design in the Victoria and Albert Museum". This three-volume work, covering the centuries from 1200 to 1940, was written by members of the Department of Textiles and Dress, edited by the then Keeper, Donald King. Intended to illustrate as many textiles and designs for textiles as possible, the book was seen as an opportunity to publish and to publicise the Museum's superb textile collections, benefitting from the excellent colour photography of Takahiko Sano and the renowned quality of Gakken's publications. One slight drawback was the concomitant need to satisfy the Japanese market, interested mainly in design as repeating patterns rather than those with a pictorial element or textiles designed as complete objects, as tapestries, carpets, sets of hangings, covers, or, in the case of printed textiles, as shawls or handkerchiefs. It is hoped that these aspects of textile art will be the subject of future publications.

Natalie Rothstein wrote the section entitled "Printed Textiles to 1750" in the first volume of "British Textile Design in the Victoria and Albert Museum". There she related how, in emulation of imported Indian 'chints', fine cottons painted and printed in exquisite colours fast to washing, English manufacturers endeavoured to discover how to print mordants to interact with dyes. Before William Sherwin's patent of 1676 for 'the only true way of East Indian printing and stayning', printing on any type of cloth was with ordinary printer's ink or the paints used for 'stained cloths'. Sherwin probably discovered thickeners necessary to print metallic oxides of alum and iron, mordants to produce in one madder dye bath shades of pink, red, purple, brown and black.[I] Weld was also mordanted if a fast yellow was required. Blue, because of problems with indigo oxidising, was produced in India by laborious resist-dyeing not favoured in England. At some time in the 1730s, a method of preparing indigo was discovered that enabled it to be applied with a paint brush, 'pencilling' in small areas to add to the design already printed in madder colours and yellow, making green with the latter (see Glossary: pencilling). By 1742 'china blue' (see Glossary) had been invented, giving beautiful fast blues, but by a technique that could not be used with those needed to add other colours.[II]

Few English printed textiles can be dated before 1750. Much of our evidence for dating printing techniques and patterns in that period comes from orders preserved in the USA, sometimes with samples attached, as in the 1726 and 1749 Alexander papers.[III] Natalie Rothstein quotes the invoice book of John Bannister of Newport, Rhode Island,[IV] who was ordering china blue printed calicoes in 1742, to show how designs ordered in 1746 reflected current designs for silks: Bannister ordered a 'fine chintz silk pattern' and another with 'mosaic ground' "just at the time when figured grounds were coming into silks".[V] Three block-printed samples dated 1746 to 1748 in the album of dress fabrics of Barbara Johnson [VI] (Frontispiece, Plate 1), on the same page as a woven silk sample, show how the former might rival the latter in beauty and complexity of floral design. By 1750 the block-printing of textiles was a fine art.

NOTES

I. Peter Floud, 'The origins of English calico printing", *Journal of the Society of Dyers and Colourists*, 76, May 1960, pp. 275-281.

II. Peter Floud, "The English contribution to the early history of indigo printing", *Journal of the Society of Dyers and Colourists*, 76, June 1960, pp. 344-349.

III. Illustrated in Florence Montgomery. "Printed Textiles: English and American cottons and linens, 1700-1850", Thames and Hudson, 1970, pp. 19, 23.

IV. Newport Rhode Island, Historical Society, Invoice Book of John Bannister.

V. Natalie Rothstein, "Printed Textiles to 1750", "British Textile Design in the Victoria and Albert Museum", Vol. I, "The Middle Ages to Rococo (1200-1750)", Gakken Co. Ltd. Tokyo, 1980, pp. xxx-xxxi.

VI. Since the publication of the Gakken volumes, the album T.219-1973 has been published in facsimile by the Victoria and Albert Museum, with accompanying essays. Natalie Rothstein, ed., "Barbara Johnson's Album of Fashion and Fabrics", Thames and Hudson, 1987. Chapter 3, pp. 29-35, "Textiles in the Album' by Natalie Rothstein.

THE PATTERN-DRAWERS AND THEIR TRADE

THE DESIGNER'S TASK

An 18th century guide to apprenticeship stated of printed-calico designing: "This requires a fruitful Fancy, to invent new Whims to please the changeable Foible of the Ladies"... "It requires no great Taste in Painting, nor the Principles of Drawing... and if a Boy is found to have any scrawling Disposition, he may be bound as soon as he has learned to read and write"[1].

Some forty years later Charles O'Brien, himself a pattern-drawer, thought the trade more exacting: "a good Pattern-Drawer... possesses a fertility of invention... He should likewise have a knowledge of the business in every stage of its process, and... how every intended effect may be obtained."[2] This was important in an industry which depended largely on brilliancy of colours produced by laborious printing and dyeing processes. From the late 18th century, developments in dye technology expanded so greatly that the pattern-drawer who was to understand it all needed to be more chemist than designer.

New printing methods added scope for talent in engraved design. Shortly after 1750, printing in ink from an engraved copper plate was adapted to printing a mordant or dye by the invention of suitable thickeners. Fine engraved designs in monochrome[3] on a large scale, about three feet square, then supplemented the more colourful block-printed patterns built up, painstakingly, with numerous developing and clearing processes, from eight- to fifteen-inch blocks. In 1783 the introduction of cylinder printing, perfected in the 19th century, allowed the designer to pay less attention to the vertical joints in patterns but called for more skill in disguising lack of height in the repeat.

THE PATTERN-DRAWERS

Some designers entered the profession not as boy apprentices, but as experienced artists. The flower and bird painter, Peter Casteels, worked for calico-printers in Tooting and Richmond for the last fourteen years of his life[4]. John Baptist Jackson trained in France and Italy, where he became known for his chiaroscuro woodcuts after the works of major artists. On returning to England in 1745, he was prevailed upon to work for a calico-printer, leaving to set up a shortlived wallpaper manufactory at Battersea in 1752[5]. Jackson's designs for printed cottons were largely overlooked until Francina Irwin discovered Scottish documents of 1765 stressing their importance[6]: "Mr Jackson's principal business when in England was drawing of Patterns for the stamped Linen and Calico Trade": "he can be of very great use to that Manufacture as he understands not only the drawing but the stamping and cutting of the Blocks"[7]. He was employed in Scotland, designing and teaching apprentices, until about 1770[8].

A scrapbook containing watercolour designs and drawings associated with Jackson by inscriptions has been dismissed from Jackson's *œuvre* by Jacob Kainen[9]: yet it is difficult to see who but that artist would have sufficient interest in some humble sketches to date them, writing "Drawn from Nature... by J:B:J: at Batersea", with an occasional foreign word intruding to recall Jackson's twenty years abroad. His published work showed how he valued "true imitations of Nature". Although the scrapbook designs could be for either wallpaper or printed textiles, one in particular has a disposition of red and black outlines peculiar to printed cottons (plate 5). Until recently no surviving textiles could be attributed to Jackson. Plate 8 shows a block-printed cotton strongly analogous to his wallpapers and to motifs in the scrapbook. The classical bust in its patterned frame parallels Jackson's own description of his wallpapers, with "antique Statues... surrounded with a *Mosaic Work*, in imitation of Frames, or with Festoons and Garlands of Flowers."[10]

Casteels and Jackson were residential designers at calico-printing works, and Jackson evidently worked later to commission, being expected to design carpets and linen damasks as well as printed cottons in Scotland[11]. Some independent firms of pattern-drawers took work in such varied media. Peter de Brissac's account book of 1760-62 shows that his main employment was designing for some twenty-one silk manufacturers or mercers; but he also supplied six calico-printers or linen-drapers[12]. He charged for his designs according to the work in them. "A Mod[e]l for single purple. A Small Running figure." cost £1.10s. 0d., whereas "a Damask g[roun]d Chintz with Stripes" was £2.12s. 6d. There was further payment for putting the design on the blocks ready for cutting; and finally a separate model was painted for the pencillers who put in blues and sometimes yellows by hand. De Brissac also took impressions from the blocks, colouring in details, either to serve as records or to be offered to the client's customers for selection, as with the 'Carlisle' pattern book[13].

Designs for woven and block-printed textiles were similar in this period. Surprisingly, de Brissac also provided pictorial copper-plate designs, charging ten guineas for one 36 x 38 inches "With Variety of Birds and Severall Sorts of Beasts". His designs had to be engraved elsewhere. Many textile-printers had their own engravers, such as "Mr. Fellionter, engraver to the linen manufactory at Martin (Merton), a most ingenious artist", whose obituary appeared in 1764[14]. He may have worked for the firm of Nixon and Amyand, who introduced the art of plate-printing on cotton into England between 1752 and 1756.

Some engravers also maintained independence from any one employer, like James Hyde, "Engraver of Copper Plates for Callico Printers", recorded in 1763[15]. Similarly, David Richards, "engraver and print-cutter" in Manchester in 1781[16] was presumably the artist who inscribed the cotton on plate 64, "Drawn and Engraved by D. Richards, Manchester". Possibly he worked for a particular employer earlier near London, moving to Manchester only with the growth of the cotton-printing industry there[17], for his name as engraver only was on a handkerchief of 1768 printed at Crayford for Peele and Simpson.

THE 'OLD MASTERS' AND FLORAL PRINTS

Very few pattern-drawers had their names printed on the textiles they designed, and this useful practice occurred only on plate-printed furnishings and handkerchiefs. Even most famous designers of block-printed cottons are now only a name, with no work that can be attributed to them. In evidence given before a Parliamentary Committee in 1833, it was stated that "Raymond, Kilburn, Wagner and Edwards are regarded as the old Masters of the English school of design in calico printing"[18]. Of Raymond and Wagner, little more is known.

Edwards was presumably John Edwards, F.S.A., a famous flower painter who contributed to exhibitions of art in London between 1766 and 1791. O'Brien, about 1790, mentioned that "some years ago, an artist of repute (Mr Edwards, F.S.A.) was employed in painting flowers... as patterns for working furniture... for the Queen'. He lived at Old Ford between 1766 and 1774, at Bow in 1783, at Mitcham and Morden in Surrey in 1790, all centres of calico-printing; and some of his signed designs for block-prints, one dated 1796, still survive. Peter Floud and Barbara Morris attributed some of the designs in the Bromley Hall pattern book to Edwards, also the printed cottons of plates 87 and 107[19].

More is known about William Kilburn, thanks to a brief biography discovered by Mrs Ada Leask and to her work on him[20]. Apprenticed to a calico-printer in Ireland at an early age, he also drew patterns for wallpapers in his spare time. Coming to London, he sold designs for calicoes, and engravings to the print shops, and was employed by William Curtis, the botanist, to engrave plants for the *Flora Londinensis*[21]. Offered a partnership by a calico-printer at Wallington in Surrey, he was able to buy out his partner in seven years. The excellence of his designs, the high quality of his printing and his shrewd business sense caused his printworks to flourish when many others went bankrupt. Charles O'Brien, who described himself as "late designer to Mr Kilburn" in 1792, revealed how other firms competed for Kilburn's services: "Lay and Adams offered 500 l. per annum to draw for them" in 1785-86, and Livesey, Hargreave, Anstie, Smith and Hall tried to tempt him into their already over-partnered firm in 1788.

Kilburn maintained his independence; although, like most calico-printers, having a close financial dependence on the drapers who sold his goods. O'Brien discussed the relationship of designers and manufacturers to these retailers: "It often happens... that many (Drapers particularly) are violent in requiring something new or totally different from what has ever been seen". If too radical a change in style was mooted, O'Brien asserted "it has not a chance of getting into vogue... except where a Draper of eminence... is determined to push what is a favourite of his". Such a draper was Richard Ovey, who wrote on a design of 1799 "R. Ovey's favourite pattern (do it well)"; the drab style in which this textile was printed then coming into fashion for the next twelve years (plate 110). The instructions written on the back of one of Kilburn's designs (plate 84) may represent second thoughts from Kilburn to his printers, but more probably originated from the Drapers Brown, Rogers & Co, named on many of his designs. Their co-operation was fruitful. O'Brien stated that Kilburn's designs were so fine that "no other Printer could or would execute them; and no other Draper, but he for whom they were done, would have dared to engage them" (e.g. plates 72, 77, 81, 82).

A volume of these designs, some with dates between 1787 and 1792, has recently come to light (plates 68-84). We can be certain that these were not the work of O'Brien for Kilburn, because the former confessed that he "seldom affected... exquisite neatness of drawing". Besides employing O'Brien, Kilburn encouraged artistic initiative from his workmen, offering annual premiums for the best designs[22].

Apart from the excellence of his designs and printing, Kilburn gave great service to the trade by securing copyright on designs for three months[23]. This pleased the London printers, who tended to deal in original designs for the quality market, and displeased manufacturers in the North, who produced more for the "lower Class of People" and depended on cheaper copies of London fashions[24]. Kilburn's products at 6s. 9d. a yard could be copied by Peel & Co. at Bury and in only ten days be flooding the London shops at 4s. 6d. a yard. O'Brien feared cut-price methods would lose the custom of "persons of taste, fashion and opulence" who would not want at five or six shillings what their servants could buy in imitation for two or three.

DESIGNING IN THE 19TH CENTURY

The copyright law was maintained through the early 19th century, and in 1833 the Manchester printers, who had by then virtually taken over the industry, leaving London with little more than the printing of handkerchiefs, themselves appreciated the protection of the copyright law, seeking to have it extended to six months because "the protection ceases long before the termination of the season"[25]. Despite increasing sales of quite expensive furnishing cottons to the Royal Household from 1795 to 1815, the increase in cylinder- or roller-printing and the introduction of steam-power were leading the trade inexorably towards a wider market. The repeal of the Excise Duty in 1831 made goods for home consumption 30-40 per cent cheaper. Thomson of Clitheroe stated that a printed cotton produced in 1795 for 2s. 3d. a yard would in its 1833 equivalent cost only 8d.

At the beginning of the century, the pattern-drawers' trade was largely unaltered. The linen-drapers commanded patterns from the designers, a few of whose names are found on designs for block-prints used by the Crayford printers and at Bannister Hall. John Polley, G. Rivers, J. J. Pearman, J. Scott Jnr. and 'Rolf' produced designs in the current classical and Egyptian tastes; and the rather more talented Daniel Goddard drew powerful floral designs[26]. These have heavy black outlines to one side of each leaf or stem, giving the effect of a cast shadow[27]. But as work for the pattern-drawer increased with the greater market, he lost all identity, existing only as a nameless part of a northern printworks or influential firm of engravers such as Joseph Lockett of Manchester. One exception was a London firm established before 1790 by

Thomas Vaughan, pattern-drawer and print-cutter, still flourishing as Vaughan and Sons in 1835, apparently on a postal trade (plates 152-172).

In 1837 there was an attempt to improve quality by setting up Schools of Design. Unfortunately the Manchester School, intended chiefly for printed cotton designers, was described in 1849 as a most signal failure. Mr Lockett did not think it had increased artistic knowledge; while a Glasgow printer stated "I have scarcely seen a pattern produced entirely by the Schools of Design, that we could work". He confessed: "The French lead the taste and we follow them. I go to Paris three or four times a year for no other purpose than to buy designs and see what the French are doing"[28]. What a contrast from Mortimer's proud assertion of 1763: "those who are not, by a false taste, servilely attached to foreign commodities, must ever give the preference to an English printed cotton, for the regularity of its design and its masterly execution"[29].

THE PATTERNS: ELEGANCE IN PRINTED TEXTILES, 1750 TO 1800

IMITATIONS

The prevailing fashions in printed cottons in the 1740s and 1750s were described in *The Laboratory or School of Arts*[30]. "With respect to drawing of patterns for the calico-printers, they are for the generality in imitation after the fashions of the flowered silk-manufactory... the whole chintz... can imitate the richest silk brocades, with a great variety of beautiful colours: these make the best appearance on an open white ground. The fashion of late, as with the brocaded silks, has run upon natural flowers, stalks and leafs, sometimes intermixt with ornaments after the *French* taste;" (plate 4), "sometimes in groupes or festoons of flowers or fruit," (plate 5), "and sometimes in sprigs and branches carelessly flung, ranged or dispersed in a natural and agreeable manner" (plates 3, 6-7, 16).

This preponderance of natural flowers on white grounds is borne out by surviving chintzes and designs of the period, the patterns of John Baptist Jackson (plates 3-7), the dress samples of Barbara Johnson (Frontispiece plate 1, plate 34) and the samples taken to France about 1750 by the industrial spy, John Holker[31]. There was, however, considerable variation in the grounds available, fancy ones, as in three of the thirteen Holker samples and Barbara Johnson's dress of 1752 (plate 34), or coloured. The *Laboratory* named black, chagreen, blue and cloth colour. The two latter were popular with part of the pattern "preserved in paste in imitation of a silk tobine". De Brissac, who as a designer of woven silks could readily adapt their designs to printed textiles, sold models in 1760 for "A Chintz Tobine" and "A Damask g[roun]d". His account book reveals an increase in dark grounds in 1761 and coloured grounds in 1762. The fashions for these grounds were no doubt encouraged to fluctuate seasonally in order to promote sales.

The *Laboratory* listed five main types of printed cotton; "whole chintzes" with three reds, two purples, blue, green and yellow, which would be blended to produce crimson, orange, olive, buff and chocolate; "half-chintz", having these colours less two reds and the purples; "five-colour chintz", with only one red "and a black outline for all the rest of the colours, as blue, green and yellow"; and "last of all are the single purples". De Brissac sold patterns for most of these combinations, and many "2 purples" in 1760 and 1762. The patterns of these "common or Coarse cottons" were probably fairly simple, like Barbara Johnson's two-purple gown of 1760 (plate 35). Her scrapbook proves that coarse cottons (plates 38, 102) with minimal or very crude designs (also plates 36, 39, 100), which might have been thought suitable for linings or for servants' wear, supplemented the rich silks and elaborately printed cottons of a moderately fashionable and wealthy woman.

The *Laboratory* in 1756 noted of the three-colour patterns: "some work of this kind has been done on fine cottons, in imitation of needle-work... very much admired and wore by ladies of the first rank and fashion, for a dishabille or undress". De Brissac provided "Models for Black and Red in the Needlework Taste" in 1762. Plate 17 shows a full chintz design, the flower petals filled with tiny "stitches", imitating an Indian embroidery. Similar markings appear in a monochrome plate-impression in the Bromely Hall pattern book, among the designs taken over from Robert Maxwell in 1783 (plate 14).

Brocades, tobines, damasks and embroideries were not the only techniques imitated in printed cottons. Plate-printing suggesting 'clouded' silks embellished a design or created striking patterns (plates 29, 88). Richard Ovey sold "pink and green cloud Call[icoe]s" to the Prince of Wales in 1791-92[32]. Indian painted palampores inspired the bizarre fillings in plant forms (plates 30, 32, 89, 108), and their tree designs were reproduced as repeating patterns (plates 89, 110). Chinese painted silks and wallpapers were copied in a Bromley Hall pattern and in a 'slight chintz' of 1748 (plate 2).

CHINOISERIE, ROCOCO, AND THE SURVIVAL OF SINUOUS FORM

Chinoiserie appeared in block-printed textiles with figures influenced by Edward's and Darly's *New Book of Chinese Designs* in 1754 (plate 18), and flourished in plate-prints. Nixon & Co copied scenes from Pillement's *Livre de Chinois*, 1758: Bromley Hall patterns included "Pagoda" and "Chinese Figures"[33]. John Baptist Jackson disdained chinoiserie – "Lions leaping from Bough to Bough like Cats... Men and Women, with every other Animal, turn'd Monsters, like the Figures in a Chinese Paper" – seeking instead "Harmony and Repose, and true Imitations of Nature in Drawing and Design"[34]. This led him to shun the wilder excesses of the Rococo. Plate 8 abounds in C-scrolls, but they are symmetrically placed to build a harmonious whole, lent a rococo touch by the asymmetry of flower garlands and dissimilar birds.

Rococo sometimes ran riot in printed textiles (plates 11, 15), but more frequently took a mild English form, the serpentine line of Hogarth's Line of Beauty (plates 6, 7, 16, 42-45). In the 1760s a less subtle meander was in fashion, following French silks with elaborate 'laces' (plates 28, 31, 32). When in the 1770s silks passed from curves to stripes, printed stripes were fewer but more varied and inventive (plates 24, 25, 29, 30); and when silk designs were tending to decrease in size, printed cotton fashions maintained both large and small patterns[35]. Indeed, an exceptional dress of plate-printed cotton at Snowshill Manor,

Gloucestershire, with a 3-foot repeat of the *Story of Telemachus* was made after 1774 since it has blue threads in the selvedges[36].

The most successful patterns of the late 1770s were sizeable floral trails which seem to have lasted into the 1790s. The printed garment trade, like that of woven silks, was seasonal. O'Brien even attributed the bankruptcy of the printers Lay and Adams to their failure to complete a season's orders on time. Yet the same elements, a spiky-leaved floral trail with a vermicular ground, are found both in Barbara Johnson's dress of 1779 and in a design on paper watermarked 1794[37]; and three patterns from the 'Carlisle' pattern book exist in an appliqué quilt dated 1780, while one 'Carlisle' design recurs in a Scottish copy of the 1790s[38]. No doubt the infinite variations possible on this graceful theme (plates 41-47, 37, 33, 48-51,), helped by alternative grounds (plates 41-44) sustained public demand.

FLORAL STYLISATION AND NATURALISM

The exotic "Indian" flowers, the fantastic after Pillement (plates 19, 57) and decorative stylisation vied with 18th century delight in truth to nature represented by the flowers of Jackson, Edwards and Kilburn. The latter's botanical illustrations in *Flora Londinensis* were used by calico-printers like Joseph Talwin of Bromley Hall to create superb plate-printed furnishings (plate 66). Kilburn's polychrome floral designs were exceptional for their delicacy. His dated patterns in the late 1780s show some stylisation and strong ground colour contrasts (plate 77): in 1790 naturalism pre-dominated, with fragile flowers offset by skeletal leaves (plate 69), fern, roots (plate 68) or seaweed (plate 70). Many of these designs were on white grounds, although O'Brien stressed in 1790 "dark or shady patterns (according to the present humour)", and mentioned a popular dark ground pattern "with a kind of moss or spray hanging down in great quantities" (plates 68, 98). He wrote of Kilburn, "His patterns for 1790 run chiefly on an imitation of sea weed" (plates 70, 81, 82). Kilburn's biographer stated that he presented a piece of muslin chintz "the sea-weed pattern, designed by himself, to her Majesty Queen Charlotte".

In 1791 seaweed and coloured compartments were still prominent, but tended to be arranged in stripes (plates 81, 82, 84). This was the height of fashion, five of the nine named patterns purchased for the Royal Household in that year being striped. Many striped floral cottons survive from the 1790s (plates 90-94). Kilburn's amazingly colourful furnishing designs, one dated 1792, also included stripes (plates 72, 73).

O'Brien listed several simple colour combinations of around 1790; black and orange, buff and blue "lately much in request" and "the black, dove and yellow stile". At the end of the century drabs came into fashion, encouraged by the expiry of Bancroft's patent for quercitron, to make "demy-chintzes" without any of the madder colours (plates 110, 128-131).

Engraved Pictorial Design

The end of the century saw also virtually the end of pictorial plate-print designs. Even when put together from many different sources, like the piece in plates 9-10, containing a scene from an etching of 1652 by Nicholas Berchem, with additional animals from illustrations by Francis Barlow and birds from an engraving of 1740[39], the cottons of the 1760s had dignity and grace. It was natural for engraved designs to be borrowed from already published sources, whether prints showing leading theatrical characters (plate 40) or the books intended as models published by Robert Sayer (plate 11). Furnishing fashions changed less quickly than those for dress, as can be seen from plate impressions in the Bromely Hall book, inscribed with the names of Talwin and Foster (1785-90) and prices indicating current stock in trade although of patterns designed some twenty years earlier (plates 11, 28).

Engraved plates could suit any taste or fancy, yet the fashion for plate-prints waned and their designs declined. The hunting scenes in plate 15, dated 1790 by an Excise stamp, makes a lamentable contrast with plates 12-13. In the 19th century cylinders superseded copper plates except for printing handkerchiefs. A brief resurgence of pictorial designs in the 1820s produced scenes similar to plate 151, overcrowded, of stunted height and lacking in artistic merit[40].

Nineteenth Century Novelties in Printed Cotton, 1800 to 1850

Taste and style, 1800 to 1815

18th century traditions in design and printing lingered in the 1800s, with a growing profusion of tastes in patterns and styles in colouring. Eclectic taste can be seen in the Bannister Hall record books and in Dudding's sample borders (plates 113-123). Classical and Gothic designs (plates 119-121) vied with contemporary pleasure in draperies and tassels (plates 116, 117) and perennial flowers. Inspiration was sought as before from India and China[41], with a new interest in Egypt. The furniture designs of George Smith[42] and Thomas Hope popularised the taste, and although Hope warned young artists never to adopt hierloglyphic figures from "a mere aim at novelty", this was disregarded in printed cottons, both Dudding and Ovey commissioning "Hieroglyphick" borders (plates 114, 115). The taste was prominent from 1804 to 1809. Gothic, with less outlandish outlines, was a more lasting fashion. It even penetrated royal circles with a gothic window blind for Princess Amelia in 1807[43]; but more favoured at court were the classical styles indiscriminately called Grecian, Etruscan or Pompeian.

Classical motifs in borders combined with a "cashmere" central filling derived from Indian shawls did not disturb artistic sensibilities (plates 112, 124). This type of filling is also found with Richard Ovey's "Needlework... Chintz Border" of 1805 (plate 125), based on counted thread embroidery patterns, particularly the newly arrived Berlin Woolwork. Printed cotton designs with jagged outlines imitating the squares of canvas were popular well into the 1830s (plates 190, 191), competing with similar outlines imitating woven shawls (plates 211, 212). Patterns from shawls lasted throughout these fifty years. Although the bizarre "Indian" flowers survived into the early 19th century (plates 126, 127), they were superseded by the pine-cone pattern which came to be known as "Paisley" from the shawls[44].

To these printed 'shams', "striving to imitate the exact appearance of threads inserted by the loom"[45], the 19th century added a mock twill weave (plate 213), an appearance of watering (plate 220) and a two-tone style, thought to be new, imitating damask[46] (plate 219, 222). In 1808 the Duke of Clarence in St James's had a "crimson damask pattern cotton" in preference to silk damask[47].

Among large-scale patterns of this period, the pillar-print was outstanding. The striped ground of the 1790s gave way to trellis and fret patterns, and the stripes developed into pillars, classical, Gothic, marbled or crazed (plates 128-130, 133, 149, 193) lasting from 1800 to 1818 and recurring in the 1830s (plate 194)[48]. In spite of the desire for novelty, certain motifs continued in popular demand for as much as thirty years. The sample books of Miles and Edwards (see plates 213-215) record sales of particular patterns over five and ten year periods, and some of their designs put on sale in the 1820s can be found in the Bannister Hall samples of 1802-07. Among these was a leopard spot, which appeared in a surprising number of variations.

Themes of 1811-15 which were not repeated were islands with little trees, combined with bridges, ruins and birds (plates 138-142). The latter were particularly numerous around 1815, often on a dipped blue or a tea-ground. Earlier in the century yellow, chocolate and scarlet grounds (plates 111, 126, 127) were favoured, with white to offset the drab style. Identical patterns are sometimes difficult to identify in the Bannister Hall books, transformed by differing styles of drab, chintz and Pompeian, the latter printed in reds and black on a dyed yellow ground (plates 112, 124).

CHEMICAL DISCOVERIES

Even in the first decade of the century, new styles based on chemical discoveries began to change the appearance of printed textiles. Discharges on dark grounds with startlingly white patterns emphasised by pin-dots were improved by new discharge methods to the standards of plates 132-134. The first fast single green (plates 146, 147), patented in 1809, led to numerous other solid greens not needing blue placed over yellow[49]. A resist for blue acting as a mordant for red brought the 'lapis style' into fleeting favour from 1808 (plates 135-137).

A form of 'dry-dyeing', printing topical colours and fixing them by steaming, introduced into Lancashire around 1813, produced a whole range of sharper colour tones, such as cochineal pink, invented in 1818, and steam blues and green based on Prussian blue. Most of the chemical discoveries were made on the continent and had to be re-invented by chemists in British printworks. John Mercer produced manganese 'bronze', a dark brown, in 1822-23. This style remained "in vogue for 8 or 10 years chiefly by giving a new face to it every few months"[50]. Mercer remembered some nine new major colour combinations based on this ground between 1823 and 1831. Some of these were with chrome yellow, from which he also produced numerous styles. Chrome was all the rage of the 1820s (plates 176, 177).

The radical changes in colouring for printed cottons can be seen by comparing Barbara Johnson's dress fabrics (plates 34-39, 98-106) with those of 1824 (plates 173-184); and the differences in traditional chintz palette between the pillar prints of plates 193 and 194.

DESIGNS OF 1815 TO 1850, COTTON AND SHAWLS

A few firms, like Bannister Hall, still produced expensive block-printed furnishings, some of the most elaborate being "landscape" blinds for windows (plate 195); but the vast majority of manufacturers turned to roller-printing. Four minutes sufficed to print by machine a design that would take two people six hours to work on the same length of cotton by hand[51]. Combinations of engraved and 'surface' rollers produced the fine striped floral furnishings of plates 145-148, often with honeycomb grounds, which were in fashion around 1815-20. The fine engraving possible was exploited in the machine-grounds of the 1820s-30s (plates 191, 216, 225, 228, 231), many of which came from the cylinder making and engraving workshop of Joseph Lockett.

Dress fabrics of the 1820s, mostly small patterned (plates 152-184), included radical new designs (plate 153) and some rather retrospective, with draperies (plates 173, 174) and mossy trails (plates 157, 166, 168, 170, 180, 181). 1823 was noted at Broad Oak for romantic designs called "cloud" and "storm" with "waving moss blown by the wind"[52]. 1824 saw the introduction there of the "rainbow style" (plates 176, 177, 180, 181), which added to this effect of movement when a slanting figure crossed the blurred edges of the stripes.

In furnishings of the 1830s, Gothic remained popular, the Bannister Hall books being full of "Gothic window Chintz blinds" (plate 196). Birds flew back into fashion with the publication of Audubon's spectacular *Birds of America*[53] (plates 197, 203, 204); rococo curves were filled with strange floral devices, and sinuous 'laces' with flowers recalled the woven silks of the 1760s (plates 200, 201). A new taste was the Elizabethan, based on strapwork patterns. Plate 230 shows a cotton named 'Elizabethan' designed by the artist Thomas Willement, forerunner of the great designers who were to rescue the decorative arts from their enfeebled anonymity.

Increasingly, however, a search for new forms led to hectic, indiscriminate patterning (plates 205, 206, 232), striving for difference and falling between ugly novelties and perversions of old forms (plates 210, 233). In attempting to find new combinations, even the colours ceased to be pleasing. *The Journal of Design* summed up the sad position:

"There is a morbid craving in the public mind for novelty as *mere novelty*, without regard to intrinsic goodness... The manufacturer... cannot be content with harmonious blendings of colour, but is compelled to be most uncomplimentary in his colouring."[54] (Plates 232-234).

In contrast to this deterioration in design and colour, found in printed cottons produced increasingly by mechanical means for a mass market, hand-block printed shawls in silk and wool maintained quality, their designs evolving in seemingly limitless variety of complex and colourful patterns based largely on those of woven Indian shawls, with European embellishments (plates 235, 236). As improved weaving technology increased the size of the repeat in woven shawls, printed patterns also spread until there was no repeat in half a shawl (plate 236). A Juror's Report on the 1851 Exhibition stated that a shawl submitted by Charles Swaisland "required 550 blocks to complete the pattern. The colouring is bright and clear, the execution perfect". Some of the inspiration for Swaisland's designers came from France[55] but the excellence of his patterns, which he took care to register for copyright, helped to maintain the high standards of printed textile design prevailing in England for one hundred years.

NOTES

1. R. Campbell, *The London Tradesman*, London, 1747, pp 115-116.
2. Charles O'Brien, *The Callico Printers' Assistant*. Vol. I 1789, Vol II 1792 (written, from internal evidence, in 1790). Reprints 1792 and 1795 with different titlepages. No pagination.
3. Some plate-impressions in the Musée de l'Impression sur Etoffes, Mulhouse, are marked "Planche de cuivre en deux couleurs", from the Ware printworks at Crayford. They would have been in madder colours, as china blue could not be used with madder. Block and pencilling could of course add colour to a copperplate design (plate 12, 13).
4. Horace Walpole, *Anecdotes of Painting*. Section on Casteels, who died in 1749.
5. *An Enquiry into the Origins of Printing in Europe, by a Lover of Art*, London, 1752. Contains many biographical details of Jackson's life.
6. Francina Irwin, "Scottish Eighteenth Century Chintz and its Design", Part I, *The Burlington Magazine*, Vol. CVII, September 1965, pp. 455-456.
7. Minutes of the Board of Trustees for Improving Fisheries and Manufactures in Scotland, March 18th 1765. Register House, Edinburgh.
8. Jackson was then at least seventy years old. See biographical notes.
9. Jacob Kainen, *John Baptist Jackson: 18th-Century Master of the Color Woodcut*, Washington, 1962, p. 48.
10. John Baptist Jackson, *An Essay in the Invention of Engraving and Printing in Chiaro Oscuro...*, London, 1754, p. 8.
11. Minutes of the Board... in Scotland, *op. cit.*
12. Manuscript Account Book of P.A. Brissac, 1760-62. Original in the Joseph Downs Manuscript Library of the Henry Francis Dupont Winterthur Museum, Delaware. Photocopy in the V & A Library.
13. Victoria and Albert Museum, Department of Prints and Drawings, E.1348 to E.2008-1921. Now in mounts, but originally bound with a label exhorting the customer to keep the book clean and return it promptly because 'the Patterns have cost a good deal of Money'.
14. *The Gentleman's Magazine*, Vol. XXXIV, 1764, p. 147.
15. T. Mortimer, *The Universal Director...*, London, 1763.
16. Manchester Directory for 1781. His name is missing from other Manchester Directories, perhaps because he did not subscribe to them.
17. Cheaper labour and the proximity of the cotton-mills attracted printers to the North, particularly around Manchester. The repeal in 1774 of the Act forbidding home use of all-cotton cloth encouraged the printing industry.
18. Evidence of James Thomson, calico-printer, of Clitheroe, Lancashire.
19. Loan Exhibition of English Chintz, Catalogue of Exhibition at the Victoria and Albert Museum, 1960. Contains the essence of the research of Peter Floud and Barbara Morris.
20. Biography of William Kilburn by I. H. in *The Dublin Penny Journal*, Vol. I, No 23, December 1st, 1832, pp. 183-184, summarised in Ada Leask, "William Kilburn and the earliest Copyright Acts for Cotton Printing Designs" in *The Burlington Magazine*, Vol. XCV, July 1953, pp. 230-233.
21. William Curtis, *Flora Londinensis*, Vol. I published 1777, Vol. II, 1798. Other artists who were major contributors were James Sowerby and Sydenham Edwards.

22. Biography of William Kilburn, *op. cit.*

23. Petition of William Kilburn, March 15th 1787 to the passing of the Act, May 1787. Commons' Journals. All details given in Ada Leask, *op. cit.*

24. Petition of Calicoe Manufacturers and Printers in the County of Lancashire. Commons' Journals, April 25th 1787.

25. Evidence of calico-printer James Thomson of Primrose, Clitheroe, to a Parliamentary Committee on Commerce and Manufactures. Reports to Committees vol. VI. Session January 29th to August 29th, 1833, para. 3859.

26. Peter Floud, "The Drab Style and the Designs of Daniel Goddard" in *The Connoisseur*, Vol. CXXXIX, May 1957, pp 234-239. Barbara Morris, "The Classical Taste in English Wood-block Chintzes" in *The Connoisseur*, Vol. CXLI, March 1958, pp. 93-97.

27. Florence Montgomery, *Printed Textiles: English and American Cottons and Linens 1700-1850*, p 135, attributes the textile on plate 109 to Goddard on the strength of its thick outlines; but in this case they are uniform and do not have the characteristic 'shadow' effect. The book is excellent on the sources of designs.

28. Reports to the Commons Committee on the Schools of Design, given in *The Journal of Design*, Vol. 2, Sept. 1849, p. 27 ff. James Thomson confessed in 1833 that he went to France to look for patterns; but stated, too, that a leading French calico-printer had just come to London to do the same.

29. T Mortimer, *The Universal Director*, London 1763.

30. Godfrey Smith, *The Laboratory or School of Arts*, London Vol. II, 1756. Section, which appears only in this edition, "Of designing and drawing of ornaments... for the use of the flowered-silk manufactory, embroidery, and printing."

31. Florence Montgomery, "English Textile Swatches of the Mid-Eighteenth Century" in *The Burlington Magazine*, Vol. CII, June 1960; and "John Holker's Mid-Eighteenth Century *Livre d'Echantillons*" in *Studies in Textile History. In Memory of Harold B. Burnham*, Toronto, 1977, pp. 214-231.

32. Public Record Office, HO 73/22. Bundle marked Richard Ovey. 1791, November 20th "84 yds ell wide Pink and green cloud Calls. 5/3."

33. "The Loan Catalogue of English Chintz", *op. cit.*, and Florence Montgomery, *Printed Textiles*, *op. cit.*, contain many useful details concerning design.

34. John Baptist Jackson, *An Essay on the Invention of Engraving and Printing in Chiaro Oscuro*, London, 1754.

35. The samples from Barbara Johnson's scrapbook are not representative as regards size, being chosen to show repeats where possible.

36. When printing on all-cotton cloth was allowed in 1774, three blue threads had to be woven into the selvedges to identify the cloth of English manufacture for paying Excise Duty. This regulation was repealed in 1811.

37. Victoria and Albert Museum, Department of Prints and Drawings, E.39-1964.

38. Francina Irwin, *op. cit.*

39. Loan Catalogue of English Chintz, 1960, cat. No. 84.

40. Peter Floud, "Pictorial Prints of the 1820s" in *Antiques*, Vol. LXXI, November 1957, pp. 455-459.

41. Dudding's book contains both chinoiserie and exact copies of motifs found in Chinese silks and embroidery.

42. George Smith, *A collection of Designs for Household Furniture*, London, 1826, relates how the taste came into fashion.

43. Public Record Office L.C. 11. 10.

44. *The Journal of Design*, on an exhibition of the Manufactures at the Society of Arts, 1850, p. 80.

45. *The Journal of Design*, Vol 4, 1850, pp. 8-10, "Shams and Imitations".

46. Praised as a new 'chaste' style in Ackermann's *Repository*, January 1890.

47. Public Record Office, L.C. 11.10.

48. Peter Floud, "The pillar print" in *Antiques*, October 1957, pp. 352-355.

49. Lightfoot of Broad Oak produced one early in the 1830s, leading to a crop of floral cottons "with large green leaves". Benjamin Hargreaves wrote of his work in *The Journal of Design*, Vol. 3, 1850, in the articles on Hargreaves Calico Print Works at Broad Oak, Accrington (pp. 5-9, 44-47, 77-80); claiming for Lightfoot some of the discoveries attributed to Mercer.

50. Notes given by John Mercer of Oakenshaw through his son to the Royal Society, transcribed by John Graham in his manuscript notes of 1846, now in Manchester Public Library. This style could be purchased quite cheaply after its novelty wore off. James Thomson gave evidence in 1833 that seven yards of "A bronze ground, with a white discharge or a yellow discharge upon it" purchased for a dress would total 1s. 9d., ie. 3d a yard.

51. *A complete History of the Cotton Trade, including... Calico-Printing*, by a Person concerned in Trade, Manchester, 1823, p. 164.

52. Article on Broad Oak, *op. cit.*, note 49.

53. Separate plates were issued in 1827, the first complete volume in 1830. Discussed in detail in Barbara Morris, "Audubon's Birds of America" In *Antiques*, Vol. LXXI, December 1957, pp. 560-563, where she attributes the engraving of the rollers to John Potts of New Mills, Derbyshire.

54. "On the Multitude of New Patterns" in *The Journal of Design*, Vol. 1, March 1849, pp. 4-5.

55. Wendy Hefford, "Pattern books and Precursors" in *From East to West: Textiles from G. P. & J. Baker*, a catalogue of an exhibition held in the Victoria and Albert Museum, October 1984, p 30.

PLATES

Frontispiece, 1. A page, from the scrapbook made by Barbara Johnson dating from 1746 to 1828, with three block-printed samples (see also plates 34-49, 98-106).

TOP LEFT: "a flower'd Calicoe" 1746. A full chintz in reds, purples, yellow and blue overprinted for green, orange and brown with a floral design comparable in style to the brocaded silk lower on the page (bottom left).

SECOND LEFT: "a flower'd Cotten" 1747. A five colour chintz, red, black, blue and yellow making green, with the ground colour reserved round the floral design, like woven silks with a patterned ground that is voided round the brocaded areas.

SECOND RIGHT: "a blue and white Linnen" 1748. This is the earliest known dated example of china blue. It is printed on linen, and the other two samples, though called 'calico' and 'cotton' by their owner, were printed on fustians of linen warp and cotton weft to avoid breaking the law against printing on cotton, in force until 1774 in response to the demands of the woollen and silk industries.
T.219-1973

2. Paper pattern of a printed textile; imitation of Chinese painted silk. Dated on the back, June 30th 1748.
Block-impression in red and black with additional painted colour.
16³/₈ x 11³/₄ in. (41.5 x 30 cm)
Numbered 1741 on the front, with the inscription: "for slight Chintz shaded Red. Linnens Cottons & Callicoes".
E.141-1964.

3. Design for a printed textile. By John Baptist Jackson, between 1745 and 1755.
Watercolour with some preliminary pencil.
17¹/₂ x 12¹/₂ in. (44.5 x 31.7 cm)
E.4487-1920.

4. Design for printed textile or wallpaper; flowers and strapwork. By John Baptist Jackson, between 1745 and 1755.
Watercolour.
13¹/₂ x 18 in. (34.2 x 45.7 cm)
E.4534-1920.

5. Design for a printed textile. By John Baptist Jackson, between 1745 and 1755.
Watercolour with some pencil.
13¹/₂ x 18¹/₂ in. (34.2 x 47 cm)
E.4529-1920.

6-7. Paper pattern (in two parts) of a printed textile; naturalistic flowers. Designed by John Baptist Jackson, between 1745 and 1755.
Block-impression on paper.
(Total) 25¹/₂ x 18 in. (64.7 x 45.7 cm)
E.4533, E.4538-1920.

8. Furnishing chintz; rococo ornament and birds, with a bust and an urn. Probably designed by John Baptist Jackson, about 1750.
Block-printed cotton, with pencilled blue.
Repeat, 34 ³/₄ x 36 in. (88.2 x 91.4 cm)
The repeat is made to seem twice this height by putting the bust in alternate repeats to the urn.
T.243-1979 .

9-10. Plate-printed furnishing; pastoral scene, birds and ruins. Printed by Robert Jones & Co., Old Ford, Middlesex, 1761.
Cotton printed from two engraved copper plates.
Repeat, 80 x 34 in. (203 x 86.3 cm)
Inscribed: "R. I. & Co. Old Ford 1761" and "R. IONES 1761".
Pastoral scene, animals and birds are taken from published works of the 17th and 18th centuries.
442-1897.

11. Paper-impression of a printed textile; "Peacock", with rococo scrolls. Printed at Bromley Hall, Middlesex, about 1765.
Plate-printed.
20¹/₂ x 26 in. (52 x 66 cm)
The peacock is taken from A New Book of Birds published by Robert Sayer, London, 1765, probably drawn by Charles Fenn. Plates are taken from designs used at Bromley Hall between about 1760 and 1800, bound together after 1790. The copper-plate designs are mostly larger than the sheets of paper on which they are printed. Plate 67 shows that the manufacturers sometimes used cotton also too narrow for the design.
E.458(210, 211)-1955.

12-13. Plate-printed furnishing; shooting and fishing scenes. Printed by Robert Jones & Co., Old Ford, Middlesex, 1769. Linen and cotton printed in purple from two engraved plates, with other colours added by woodblock and blue by pencilling.
Repeat, 81½ x 36½ in. (207 x 92.7 cm)
Inscribed: "R. IONES & Co. Old Ford" and
"R. IONES & Co. Iany. 1st 1769".
T.140-1934.

14. Plate-impression from the Bromley Hall pattern book. 1760s-1770s.
E.458(38)-1955.

15. Cotton plate-printed china blue at Bromley Hall. 1760s-1770s.
T.137-1956.

16. Design for a printed textile; naturalistic flowers in opposing curves. Late 1740s or early 1750s.
Watercolour on paper.
13 x 9½ in. (33 x 24 cm)
Inspired by silk designs of about 1747-49.
7275.106.

17. Design for a printed textile; imitation of embroidery. 1750s or 1760s.
Watercolour on paper.
16½ x 12 in. (42 x 30.5 cm)
7275.39.

18. Paper pattern of a printed textile; flowering stem with Chinamen. 1760s or 1770s.
Block-impression with additional colour by hand.
21⅛ x 16¾ in. (53.5 x 42.5 cm)
Inscribed: "No 408 at 26d". From the same pattern book as plates 128, 130-142.
E.1405-1921.

19. Design for a printed textile; rocaille and fantastic flowers. 1760s or 1770s.
Watercolour and ink.
14¾ x 12 in. (37.5 x 30.5 cm)
7275.40.

20-23. Designs for printed textiles, probably for dress materials. 1760s or 1770s.
Watercolour and ink.

20. Small floral sprig and trail in red and green.
3¾ x 4 in. (9.5 x 10.2 cm)
7275.340.

21. Small spot pattern in red and black.
4 x 3¼ in. (10.2 x 8.2 cm)
7275.339.

22. Polychrome floral sprig and meander.
3 in. (7.5 cm) square.
7275.338.

23. Trail of small, slightly stylised flowers, polychrome.
12 x 9 in. (30.5 x 22.8 cm)
Inscribed on the back with the name of the linen drapers "Peele & Simpson".
7275.341 .

24. Paper pattern of a printed textile; angular stems and opposed meander stripes. 1770s.
Block-impression with added colour by hand.
15 x 8¾ in. (38.1 x 22.2 cm)
E.1557-1921.

25. Design for a printed textile; elaborate, varied stripes. 1760s.
Watercolour and ink.
8⅛ x 10 in. (20.7 x 25.4 cm)
7275.204.

26. Patchwork of printed textiles cut to a shell or scale shape. From a set of bed hangings, third quarter of the 18th century. Mostly block-printed, some with resist for dyeing; a few painted cottons from India.
Height of large lozenge, 22 in. (55.8 cm)
Small patterned dress fabrics made excellent patchworks. The components could date from several decades earlier if old materials were used.
T.242-1908.

27. Detail of plate 193.

28. Paper-impression of a printed textile design, "P.50"; lace meanders and flowers. Printed at Bromley Hall, Essex, late 1760s or early 1770s. Plate-printed.
19¹/₂ x 24¹/₂ in. (49. 5 x 62.2 cm)
The design is inspired by woven silks of the 1760s. Paper inscribed: "P.50" "Talwin & Foster 8d."
E.458(74, 75)-1955.

29. Paper-impression of a printed textile design, "P. 163"; fancy stripes and imitation chiné. Printed at Bromley Hall, Middlesex, 1770s or early 1780s.
Plate-printed.
10 x 25 in. (25.4 x 63.5 cm)
E.458(20, 21)-1955 .

30. Paper-impression of a printed textile design, "P.166"; fancy stripes and fantastic flowers. Printed at Bromley Hall, Middlesex, 1770s or early 1780s.
Plate-printed.
10 x 25 in. (25.4 x 63.5 cm)
E.458(22, 23)-1955.

31. Paper-impression of a printed textile design, "P.51"; lace with floral trails. Printed at Bromley Hall, Middlesex, 1770s.
Plate-printed.
19¹/₂ x 24¹/₂ in. (49.5 x 62.2 cm)
E.458(68, 69)-1955.

32. Design for a printed textile; 'lace' stripe and meander, with fantastic flowers. For printing by John Munns, Crayford, Kent, 1760s or 1770s. Watercolour and ink.
12 x 18¹/₂ in. (30.5 x 47 cm)
Inscribed: "John Munns No A1064", "Cutt Compleat", "Cutt print Compleat D(ark) Red, 2 purple grounds 1 pale red do."
7275.297 ·

33. Printed linen; flowers in bunches. About 1770-74.
Block-printed, with pencilled blue.
Repeat, 22³/₄ x 12¹/₄ in. (58 x 31 cm)
Probably for a dress. The linen is very fine.
T.227-1931.

34-39. Fragments of printed dress materials, dated 1752 to 1781. From the scrapbook made by Barbara Johnson from 1746 to 1823. (See frontispiece plate 1 and plates 98-106)
T.219-1973

From right to left the fragments were described by their owner as:

34. "Two Purple and white Cotten Shepertee's the same 1752".
2⁵/₈ x 3 in. (6.7 x 7.6 cm), p.3.

35. A Purple & white Cotten Gown May 1760 half a Crown a yard".
1 ³/₈ x 3 in. (3.5 x 7.6 cm), p.8.
This has a linen warp and cotton weft.
36. "a yellow and white strip'd linnen Gown... three shillings a yard... May 1766".
3¹/₄ x 1⁷/₈ in. (8.2 x 4.7 cm), p.10.

37. "a Chintz Gown", "May 1779".
2⁷/₈ x 7¹/₂ in. (7.3 x 19 cm), p. 21.

38. "a Callicoe Gown,... ell wide, five shillings a yard September 1780.
3¹/₂ x 3 in. (8.9 x 7.6 cm), p.25.

39. "a Red and white Chintz Gown... yard wide three shillings a yard May 1781".
2³/₄ x 2³/₈ in. (7 x 6 cm), p.25.

40. Plate-printed furnishing; "Lethe, or Aesop in the Shades". Between 1766 and 1774.
Linen and cotton plate-printed in china blue.
Repeat, 39 x 31¹/₂ in. (99 x 80 cm)
Scenes from the play by David Garrick with figures from prints by Gabriel Smith and A Moseley (1750). Probably designed about the time of the command performance of 1766.
T.75-1914.

41-44. Paper patterns of printed textiles; the same floral trail on different grounds. 1770s or 1780s.
Block-impressions with additional colour by hand.
Each, 11¹/₂ x 7⁷/₈ in. (29.2 x 20 cm)
E.1843-1921, E.1562-1921, E.1372-1921, E.1710-1921.

45. Paper pattern of a printed textile; fantastic floral trails. 1770s or 1780s.
Block-impression with additional colours by hand
22 x 16³/₄ in. (55.8 x 42.5 cm)
E.1403-1921.

46. Paper pattern of a printed textile; floral trails on vermicular ground. 1770s or 1780s.
Block-impression with additional colour by hand.
16½ x 14⅜ in. (42 x 36.5 cm)
Similar in style to plate 37, a fragment of ell wide chintz purchased in May 1779.
E.1380-1921.

47. Paper pattern of a printed textile; floral trails on black ground. 1770s or 1780s.
Block-impression with additional colour by hand.
13⅝ x 11½ in (34.5 x 29.2 cm)
E.1689-1921.

48. Printed dress material; floral trails. About 1780.
Block-printed cotton. Three blue threads in selvedge.
Repeat, 13 x 11½ in. (33 x 29.2 cm)
From a dismembered dress.
T.191A-1964.

49. Printed dress material; floral trails on vermicular ground. About 1780.
Block-printed cotton.
Repeat, 13¼ x 15½ in. (33.5 x 39.3 cm)
Compare plate 37, dated May 1779.
T.94-1912.

50. Detail from a dress; floral trails on a dark ground. About 1780-90.
Block-printed cotton. No blue threads.
Repeat, 12⅜ x 23 in. (31.4 x 58.4 cm)
T.216-1966.

51. Detail from a dress; floral trails. About 1780.
Block-printed cotton. No blue threads.
Repeat, 13⅜ x 23⅛ in. (34 x 58.7 cm)
T.100-1966.

52. Detail from a dress; floral sprig imitating embroidery. About 1785.
Block-printed cotton. Blue threads in selvedge.
Repeat, 4⅝ x 4⅛ in. (11.7 x 10.5 cm)
T.274-1967.

53. Detail from a dress; flowers in stripes. About 1790.
Block-printed cotton. Blue threads in selvedge.
Repeat, 3⅜ x 3⅝ in. (8.5 x 9.2 cm)
T.286-1968.

54. Detail from a dress: floral sprig in small lattice on green and yellow ground. About 1780-90.
Block-printed cotton. Blue threads in selvedge.
Repeat, 3¾ x 3⁵/₁₆ in. (9.5 x 8.5 cm) Similar patterns on the same ground are among the designs in the pattern book E.1348 to 2008-1921.
T.296-1973.

55. Detail from a dress; seaweed stripe and narrow chiné stripe. About 1785-95.
Block-printed cotton. Blue threads in selvedge.
Repeat, 9½ x 8 in. (24.1 x 20.3 cm)
T.99-1966.

56. Dress material; stripes of flower stems, birds and baskets of fruit. Printed by Watson, Myers, Fielding & Co, Catterall, Lancashire; 1792.
Block-printed on muslin with a woven stripe.
Repeat, 9¾ x 16 in. (24.7 x 40.6 cm) including a half-drop.
Stamped at the end with the name of the firm, the words "British Muslin" and an Excise stamp with the date 1792.
T.60A-1932.

57. Printed cotton; fantastic flowers, birds and ribbons in the manner of Pillement. About 1775-85.
Block-printed on cotton. Blue threads in selvedge.
Repeat, 12¾ x 13¾ in. (32.3 x 35 cm)
When acquired, this chintz was made up as a valance, but it may originally have been used for dress.
Circ.363-1955.

58. Paper pattern for border of printed coverlet or tablecloth. 1770s or 1780s.
Block-impression with additional colour by hand.
19 x 10¼ in. (48.2 x 26 cm)
Matching the design for a centre, opposite, plate 60
E.1379-1921 .

59-63. Five paper patterns of printed textiles. 1770s or 1780s. Block-impressions with additional colour by hand.

59. Pattern for a dress or handkerchief fabric in black, yellow and white.
7³/₈ x 7¹/₄ in. (18.7 x 18.3 cm)
The textile would be printed with resist over the areas to be left white or dyed yellow.
E.1375-1921.

60. Quarter of a centre for a printed coverlet or cloth.
Radius, 9¹/₈ in. (23.2 cm)
See plate 58 for matching border.
E.1374-1921 .

61. Flowering stems on ground with a vermicular design, for a dress.
9³/₄ x 8¹/₈ in. (24.7 x 20.6 cm)
E.1378-1921.

62. Small spot design for dress or handkerchief.
2³/₈ in (6 cm) square.
E.1376-1921.

63. Bold design in black and white on a yellow ground, for dress or handkerchief.
7 x 6³/₄ in (17.8 x 17.2 cm)
E.1377-1921.

64. Plate-printed furnishing; homage to George III.
Designed by David Richards, about 1780.
Plate-printed cotton. Blue threads in selvedge.
Repeat, 34¹/₂ x 27 in. (87.7 x 68.5 cm)
Inscribed: "Drawn and Engrav'd by D. Richards Manchr."
Circ.90-1960.

65. Furnishing cotton; landscape with hunt.
Cotton plate-printed in 1790.
Dated by an Excise Stamp.
T.50-1933.

66. Paper-impression of a printed textile design, "P.30"; flowering plants. Printed at Bromley Hall, Middlesex, late 1770s into the 1780s.
Plate-printed.
19 x 24³/₄ in. (48.2 x 62.8 cm)
From plants drawn by William Kilburn for the *Flora Londinensis* of William Curtis, published in a fascicule of 1777. Inscribed on the back "Talwin & Foster 8d." Joseph Talwin of Bromley Hall was a subscriber to the above work.
E458(147,148)-1955

67. Printed cotton; meandering stems of flowers. Possibly designed by William Kilburn. Printed at Bromley Hall, Middlesex, about 1775.
Plate-printed in china blue.
Repeat, 38¹/₂ in. (98 cm) high.
The engraved plate was wider than the cloth, which is only 28¹/₄ in. (71.7 cm) wide. The plate-impression of this design in the Bromley Hall patternbook is numbered P.33 and inscribed "Talwin & Foster 8d."
Circ.91-1960.

68. Design for a printed textile; flowers with trailing roots. By William Kilburn, designer and calico printer, Wallington, Surrey; about 1790. Watercolour.
Plates 68 to 84 are from an album of Kilburn's designs made up after 1814. Some of the designs are dated, with dates from 1787 to 1792.
10¹/₄ x 7¹/₂ in. (26 x 19 cm)
E.894-1978, p.149 (a).

69. Design for a printed textile; flowers and skeletal leaves. By William Kilburn, designer and calico printer, Wallington, Surrey; about 1790. Watercolour.
14 x 10¹/₂ in. (35.5 x 26.7 cm)
E.894-1978, p.41.

70. Design for a printed textile; flowers, ferns and seaweed. By William Kilburn, designer and calico printer, Wallington, Surrey; about 1790.
Watercolour.
14 x 10¹/₂ in. (35.5 x 26.7 cm)
E.894-1978, p.17

71. Design for a printed textile; leaves of the spider plant and flowers. By William Kilburn, designer and calico printer, Wallington, Surrey; about 1790.
Watercolour.
13 ³/₄ x 10 ³/₈ in. (35 x 26.4 cm)
E.894-1978, p.19.

72. Design for a furnishing chintz. By William Kilburn, designer and calico printer, Wallington, Surrey; 1792.
Watercolour.
16 x 11 ³/₄ in. (40.6 x 29.8 cm)
Inscribed on the back: "629 24 Nov 92 B R".
The initials show the design was painted for the linen-drapers Brown, Rogers & Co.
E.894-1978, p.73.

73. Design for a furnishing chintz. By William Kilburn, designer and calico printer, Wallington, Surrey; about 1792.
Watercolour.
16 x 11³/₄ in. (40.6 x 29.8 cm)
This and the design plate 74 are in similar style to the pattern on page 76 of the Kilburn album, dated November 1792 and designed for the linen-drapers Brown, Rogers & Co..
E.894-1978, p.75.

74. Design for a chintz border. By William Kilburn, designer and calico printer, Wallington, Surrey; about 1792.
Watercolour.
8³/₄ x 16 in. (22.2 x 40.6 cm)
E.894-1978, p.71.

75. Design for a printed textile; stylised flowers in an oriental manner. By William Kilburn, designer and calico printer, Wallington, Surrey, about 1787-92.
Watercolour.
7¹/₂ x 9 ¹/₄ in. (19 x 23.5 cm)
E.894-1978, p.92(b).

76. Design for a printed textile; flowers on ground covered with leaves. By William Kilburn, designer and calico printer, Wallington Surrey; about 1787-92.
Watercolour.
9¹/₂ x 8 in. (24.1 x 20.3 cm)
E.894-1978, p.110(a).

77-80. Four designs for printed textiles. By William Kilburn, designer and calico printer, Wallington, Surrey; 1789-91.
Watercolour.

77. Flowers, leaves and grasses on dark ground with reserved white areas.
9 x 7 ¹/₂ in. (22.8 x 19 cm)
Inscribed on the back: "Brown Rogers & Co
4 Aug 1789 3/6".
E.894-1978, p.128(b).

78. Flowers, oak twigs and grasses on dark ground with reserved white areas.
9 x 7 in. (22.8 x 17.7 cm)
Inscribed on the back: "318 3/6". In the same style as plate 77, this probably also dates from 1789.
E.894-1978, p.128(a).

79. Decorative arrangement of flowering stems.
9¹/₄ x 7⁷/₈ in. (23.5 x 20 cm)
Probably about 1791.
E.894-1978, p.92(a).

80. Decorative arrangement of flowering stems, with coloured compartments.
10 x 7 ¹/₂ in. (25.4 x 19 cm)
Very close in design to page 110 (a) of the Kilburn album, dated January 1791.
E.894-1978, p.110(b).

81. Design for a printed textile; floral stripes. By William Kilburn, designer and calico printer, Wallington, Surrey; 1791.
Watercolour.
7¹/₂ x 10 in. (19 x 25.4 cm)
Inscribed on the back: "Brown Rogers & Co. July 18 1791 3/6".
E.894-1978, p.58(a).

82. Design for a printed textile; floral stripes with ground colour. By William Kilburn, designer and calico printer, Wallington, Surrey; 1791.
Watercolour.
7¹/₂ x 10 in. (19 x 25.4 cm)
Inscribed on the back: "Brown Rogers & Co.
Augt. 31 1791 3/-".
E.894-1978, p.58(b).

83. Design for a printed textile; naturalistic flowers in floral lattice. By William Kilburn, designer and calico printer, Wallington, Surrey; 1792.
Watercolour.
7¹/₂ x 10 in. (19 x 25.4 cm)
Inscribed on the back: "Brown Rogers & Co.
June 24 1792 600 3/3".
E.894-1978, p.66(b).

84. Design for a printed textile; fancy floral stripes with ground colour in compartments. By William Kilburn, designer and calico printer, Wallington, Surrey; 1791-92.
Watercolour.
7¹/₂ x 10 in. (19 x 25.4 cm)
Alternative designs are shown for the narrow stripes.
Inscribed on the back: "Leave out the Coral and take away the deep Red & cool down the other colours 4/-".
E.894-1978, p.57(b).

85. Detail from a dress; vermicular stripes and stripes of flowers with bows. 1780s.
Block-printed cotton. No blue threads.
Repeat, 14⁷/₈ in. (37.8 cm) high, half-drop repeat.
687-1884

86. Printed cotton; stripes and opposed meanders of ribbon and flowers. About 1785-95.
Block-printed cotton.
Repeat, 11¹/₄ x 6¹/₈ in. (28.5 x 15.5 cm)
T.37-1965.

87. Furnishing chintz; stripes and flowers tied by meandering ribbons. Possibly designed by John Edwards, about 1790.
Block-printed cotton with pencilled blue.
Repeat, 12⁷/₈ in. (32.8 cm) high, half-drop repeat.
T.64-1955.

88. Paper-impression (half missing) of a printed textile design, "P.120"; chiné ribbons. Printed by Robert Maxwell, Merton Abbey, about 1780-83, and later at Bromley Hall.
Plate-printed. 20 x 12¹/₂ in. (50.8 x 31.7 cm)
The axis lies through the flowers at the right. Another plate impression of this design at Mulhouse shows additional pattern at the left, and is there identified as the work of Robert Maxwell.
E.458(26)-1955.

89. Large-scale furnishing chintz; sinuous stems with stylised flowers and leaves. About 1795.
Block-printed cotton with pencilled blue.
Blue threads in selvedge.
Repeat, 31³/₄ x 19 in. (80.5 x 48.2 cm)
422-1887.

90. Furnishing chintz; stripes of roses and pillars.
About 1790.
Block-printed cotton with pencilled blue.
Blue threads in selvedge.
Repeat, 11³/₄ x 8⁵/₈ in. (29.8 x 21.9 cm)
T.2-1958.

91. Furnishing chintz; dark ground stripes with flowers and birds, light ground with lace and ribbons. About 1790.
Block-printed cotton with pencilled blue.
Blue threads in selvedge.
Repeat, 16 in. (40.6 cm) high, partial drop repeat.
Circ.96-1960.

92. Furnishing chintz; dark ground stripe with coloured leaves, floral meander with pineapple. Printed at Fordingbridge, Hampshire, about 1790.
Block-printed cotton with pencilled blue.
Blue threads in selvedge.
Repeat, 11³/₄ x 9¹/₄ in. (30 x 23.5 cm)
T.115-1927

93. Furnishing chintz; dark ground stripe with fruit, light ground with flowers, fern. About 1790.
Block-printed cotton with pencilled blue. No blue threads.
Repeat, 15⁷/₈ in. (40.3 cm) high, partial drop in width.
Circ.100-1960.

94. Furnishing chintz; narrow and broad stripes of stylised and naturalistic flowers. About 1790-95.
Block-printed with pencilled blue. Blue threads in selvedge.
Repeat, 14³/₈ in. (36.5 cm) high, half-drop repeat.
T.428-1976.

95. Patchwork quilt of printed cottons. Dated in the centre, 1797. Composed of cottons of the 1780s and 1790s.
Block-printed cottons.
119 x 110 in. (302.3 x 279.4 cm)
T.102-1938.

96. Detail of plate 95 Mainly small-patterned dress materials, similar to those in the Barbara Johnson scrapbook (plates 38-39, 98-102) with some floral trails similar to plates 42-46, 48-51.

97. Detail of plate 95, as plate 96.

98-106. Fragments of printed dress materials, dated 1789 to 1812. From the scrapbook made by Barbara Johnson from 1746 to 1823 (see frontispiece and plates 34-39)
T.219-1973

98. "ell-wide Callicoe" "Octr. 1789"
4¹/₂ x 2¹/₈ in. (11.4 x 5.4 cm), p.29.

99. "a Callicoe Gown, six yards, Twenty five shillings" "May 1792".
2⁷/₈ x 2¹/₂ in. (7.3 x 6.3 cm), p.35.
Cotton printed at Crayford, Kent. This design in three different colourways (inscribed "WH 39 at 18d.") was printed for Arbuthnot in 1795.

100. "A Brown & white Cotten Gown... Twenty pence a yard... March 1794".
3³/₄ x 1³/₄ in. (9.5 x 4.5 cm), p.37.

101. "A Callicoe Gown ell wide, three and sixpence a yard... April 1st 1796".
3⁷/₈ x 2³/₈ in. (9.5 x 4.5 cm), p.40.

102. "A Callicoe Gown ell wide, September 1796".
2³/₄ x 3³/₄ in. (7 x 9.5 cm), p.41.

103. "A Callicoe round gown... yard wide, half a crown a yard... December 1798".
3 x 4¹/₈ in. (7.6 x 10.5 cm), p.45.

104. "A blue Muslin round Gown... ell wide, three and sixpence a yard... March 1800".
3³/₈ x 3¹/₂ in. (8.6 x 8.9 cm), p.52
This pattern in these colours with the addition of a white spot at intervals is in an undated pattern-book.

105. "dark Callicoe, ell wide, 4s. 3d. a yard May 1804".
2³/₄ x 3 in. (7 x 7.6 cm), p.57.

106. "A Blue Spotted Muslin Gown ... ell wide, 2s. 2d. a yard April 1812".
3 x 2¹/₄ in. (7.6 x 5.7 cm), p.74.

107. Printed cotton; naturalistic flowers linked by serpentine ribbon, lightning flashes. Probably designed by John Edwards, about 1795.
Block-printed, with pencilled blue.
Blue threads in selvedge.
Repeat, 15⁷/₈ x 17³/₄ in. (40.5 x 45 cm)
T.25-1930.

108. Printed cotton; stylised exotic flowers on a fern or seaweed covered ground. About 1795.
Block-printed with pencilled blue. No blue threads.
Repeat, 9¹/₂ x 14³/₈ in. (24 x 36.5 cm)
Used for furnishing.
T.24-1930.

109. Furnishing chintz; dark ground with roses and jasmine. About 1800.
Block-printed cotton with pencilled blue.
No blue threads.
Repeat, 18³/₄ x 16³/₄ in. (47.6 x 42.5 cm)
Circ.493A-1956.

110. "Royal Oak and Ivy", furnishing cotton. Printed at Bannister Hall for Richard Ovey, 1799.
Block-printed cotton with pencilled blue, lacking madder colours; a 'demy' chintz.
Repeat, 20³/₈ x 17¹/₂ in. (51.8 x 44.5 cm)
The original design for this textile is inscribed "1172 R. Ovey's favourite pattern (do it well) Royal Oak and Ivy 20 July '99".
Circ.86-1960.

111. "The Scarlet Ground White Passion Flower Chintz". Printed at Bannister Hall for Richard Ovey, 1802.
Block-printed cotton with pencilled blue.
Blue threads in selvedge.
Repeat, 15¹/₄ x 17³/₄ in. (38.7 x 45.1 cm)
The original design is inscribed with the title above and "R. Ovey 10th December 1802".
Circ.334-1955.

112. Detail of a curtain; 'cashmere' filling and border in Pompeian colours. About 1804-10.
Block-printed cotton. Blue threads in selvedge.
Border repeat, 15¹/₄ in.(38.7 cm).
Filling repeat, 1⁵/₁₆ in. (3.3 cm)
T.138A-1973.

113. Sample of printed border; neo-classical design in yellow and black. Printed for Dudding, about 1804.
Block-printed cotton.
15³/₄ x 5 in. (40 x 12.7 cm)
The lower edge of this design appears separately, called 'Greek border', in a sample attached to an estimate for furnishing dated 1804 (T.111B-1962), and again in this truncated form in the Dudding pattern book. Plates 113 to 123 are from this book of borders, the stock of E. B. Dudding, 'Furniture Printer', purchased some time between 1814 and 1820 by the upholsterer George Oakley.
T.86-1964, sample No. 151.

114-115. Two samples of printed borders in the Egyptian taste. Printed for Dudding, about 1804.
Block-printed cotton.
114, 8 in. (20.3 cm) square.
115, 7³/₄ x 8 in. (19.7 x 20.3 cm)
In 1804 different borders in the same 'taste', "The Upright" and "The Bottom Hieroglyphick Bord[er]" were designed for Richard Ovey and printed at Bannister Hall.
T.86-1964, samples numbered 239, 240.

116-117. Samples of wide horizontal and narrow upright border with swags and tassels. Printed for Dudding, about 1802-14.
Block-printed cotton.
116, 8 x 6 in. (20.3 x 15.2 cm)
117, 2¹/₄ in. (5.7 cm) wide.
T.86-1964, samples numbered 64, 66.

118. Sample of printed border; intersecting arches. Printed for Dudding, about 1802-14.
Block-printed cotton.
2¹/₄ in. (5.7 cm) high. The wide version of this border sample No. 416, is 5³/₄ in. (14.6 cm) high.
T.86-1964, sample numbered 417.

119-120. Wide and narrow samples of printed border in the neo-classical taste. Printed for Dudding, about 1802-14.
Block-printed cotton.
119, 3⁷/₈ in. (9.8 cm) high.
120, 1⁷/₈ in. (4.8 cm) high.
T.86-1964, samples numbered 116, 117.

121. Sample of printed border in the gothic taste. Printed for Dudding, about 1802-14.
Block-printed cotton.
1⁵/₈ in. (4.1 cm) high. The wide version is 4³/₈ in. (11.1 cm). Other colourways are in brown and green, brown and buff.
T.86-1964, sample No. 118.

122-123. Samples of printed border; roses and hops in opposed meanders. Printed for Dudding, about 1802-14.
Block-printed cotton.
122, 5⁵/₈ in. (14.3 cm) high.
123, 2¹/₂ in. (6.4 cm) high.
Other colourways are in two reds, pink and white; yellow, green and white on black ground.
T.86-1964, samples of pattern No. 6.

124. Printed cotton border; "The Half Moon & 7 Stars Furniture". Printed at Bannister Hall for Richard Ovey, 1804.
Block-printed cotton, Pompeian style.
Blue threads in selvedge.
Repeat, 39¹/₄ in. (99.7 cm) high.
A 'shawl' or 'cashmere' sprig filling can be seen at the left.
An inscription on the original design for this border gives its name, date and proprietor, "August 22nd 1804 R. Ovey".
T.50-1956.

125. "The One Stripe Needlework Flower Pot Chintz Border". Printed at Bannister Hall for Richard Ovey, 1805.
Block-printed cotton. Blue threads in selvedge.
Repeat, 16 in. (40.6 cm) high.
There is a 'cashmere' filling on the left. The chintz has part of the stamp of Richard Ovey, Furniture Printer ... [to their Royal Highnesses the] Prince of Wales and Duke of York, London.
The original design is inscribed with the name of the border and "R. Ovey, 26th June 1805".
T.42-1925.

126. Furnishing chintz; fantastic 'Indian' flowers on scarlet ground. Probably printed at Bannister Hall, about 1805-10.
Block-printed cotton with pencilled blue.
Repeat, 11³/₄ in. (29.8 cm) high, drop repeat in width.
Similar designs, probably by the same artist, are in the Bannister Hall pattern books, about 1805 and 1809.
One is dated September 22nd 1809 and marked for Proctor & Brownlow.
Circ.496-1956.

127. Furnishing chintz; small floral meanders with elements of the 'Indian' taste. Printed at Bannister Hall for Richard Ovey, 1802.
Block-printed cotton with pencilled blue.
Repeat, 9⁷/₈ x 7⁵/₁₆ in. (25 x 18.5 cm)
The original design is inscribed "Ovey No. 84. Nov. 1802".
Circ.495-1956.

128. Furnishing 'demy' chintz; ferns and thin pillars, lattice ground. About 1805.
Block-printed cotton 'demy' in the drab style.
Repeat, 14⁷/₈ x 13³/₈ in. (37.8 x 34 cm)
Circ.224-1956.

129. Furnishing 'demy' chintz; Gothic pillars and flowers, ground with fancy filling. About 1805.
Block-printed cotton 'demy' in the drab style, with pencilled blue.
Repeat, 17¹/₄ x 17¹/₂ in. (43 .8 x 44.4 cm), half-drop.
Circ.223-1956.

130. Furnishing 'demy' chintz; pillars and hops. About 1805 .
Block-printed in the drab style.
Repeat, 15¹/₈ x 12³/₄ in. (38.4 x 32.4 cm)
Circ.225-1956.

131. Furnishing 'demy' chintz; lilac trellis. About 1805.
Block-printed in the drab style.
Repeat, 14 x 13¹/₈ in. (35.5 x 33.3 cm)
Circ.221-1956.

132. Printed cotton furnishing; flowers with pin-dot leaves on black ground. About 1805.
Block-printed discharge and colours, with pencilled blue.
Repeat, 15³/₄ in. (40 cm) high, half-drop.
Circ.229-1956.

133. Printed cotton furnishing; polychrome flowers on pin-dot pillars and scroll ground. About 1805.
Block-printed with discharge and colours, pencilled blue.
Repeat, 15³/₄ in. (40 cm) high, half-drop.
Circ.230-1956.

134. Printed cotton furnishing; flowers and ferns in pin-dot on blue ground. About 1805.
Block-printed discharge on indigo ground, dyed yellow.
Repeat, 11³/₄ x 8⁵/₈ in. (29.8 x 21.9 cm)
Circ.227-1956.

135. Printed cotton; flowers on a hatched ground in the 'lapis' style. About 1808.
Block-printed with 'resist-red' (resist to blue, mordant to red).
Repeat, 10¹/₄ x 8⁵/₈ in. (26 x 21.9 cm)
Circ.244-1956.

136. Printed cotton; flowers on a blue ground, 'lapis' style. About 1808.
Block-printed with 'resist-red' (resist to blue, mordant to red).
Repeat, 9³/₄ in. (24.8 cm) high, half-drop.
T.14-1978.

137. Printed cotton; floral meanders on pin-dot ground in the 'lapis' style. About 1808-15.
Block-printed with 'resist-red' (resist to blue, mordant to red).
Repeat, 15³/₄ x 13¹/₂ in. (40 x 34.2 cm)
Circ.243-1956.

138. Furnishing chintz; bridge and palm tree.
Printed by Peel & Co, Church, Lancashire, 1812.
Block-printed in madder colours, with pencilled blue.
Repeat, 15 in. (38 cm) high, half-drop.
Another piece of this design is stamped "PEEL & CO. CHURCH. Muslin BRITISH MANUFACTURE" "LINENS 190", with an Excise stamp for 1812.
Circ.268-1955.

139. Furnishing 'demy'; small trees and scattered flowers.
Printed at Bannister Hall for Proctor and Brownlow, 1811.
Block-printed 'demy' chintz, with pencilled blue.
Repeat, 16⁷/₈ x 13¹/₄ in. (43 x 33.5 cm)
T.230-1958.

140. 'Demy' with dipped blue ground; ruins and flowers.
Possibly by Matley & Son, Hodge, Cheshire, about 1816.
Block-printed 'demy' on a dipped blue ground.
Repeat, 11³/₄ x 17¹/₄ in. (30 x 43.8 cm)
Likely to be by the same designer and manufactory as plate 141.
T.6-1962.

141. Furnishing 'demy' with dipped blue ground; bird, tree and ruins. Printed by Samuel Matley & Son, Hodge, Cheshire, 1816. Block-printed 'demy' on a dipped blue ground.
Repeat, 15 in. (38 cm) high, half-drop.
Another piece of the same design is stamped "Saml. Matley & Son, Hodge. British Manufactory", with an Excise stamp for 1816.
Circ.267-1955.

142. Furnishing chintz; partridge and may tree. About 1815.
Block-printed in madder colours with pencilled blue on a 'tea-ground'.
Repeat, 15³/₄ in. (40 cm) high, half-drop.
Birds and trees in many variations appeared between 1814 and 1816.
T.394-1966.

143. Furnishing chintz; French marigold and other flowers. About 1815.
Block-printed in madder colours with pencilled blue on a tea-ground.
Repeat, 15³/₄ in. (40 cm) high, half-drop.
Circ.352B-1955.

144. Printed centre for a quilt or cover; flowers in an oval. About 1815.
Block-printed in madder colours with pencilled blue.
18 x 25³/₄ in. (45.7 x 65.3 cm)
Circ.606-1956.

145. Printed cotton furnishing; stripes of leaves and flowers on honeycomb ground. Printed by Samuel Matley & Son, Hodge, Cheshire, 1818.
Roller-printed, with Ilett's green.
Repeat, 13 x 9¹/₈ in. (33 x 23.1 cm)
Apart from samples in Ackermann's *Repository*, 1810, plates 145 to 147 are some of the earliest known samples of Ilett's single green, patented in 1809.
Circ.248-1956.

146. Printed cotton furnishing; undulating stripes of flowers honeycomb ground. Printed by Samuel Matley & Son, Hodge, Cheshire, 1818.
Roller-printed, with Ilett's green.
Repeat, 14 x 9¹/₄ in. (35.5 x 23.5 cm)
Circ.247-1956.

147. Printed cotton furnishing; pansies in a leafy stripe honeycomb ground. Printed by Samuel Matley & Son, Hodge, Cheshire, 1818.
Roller-printed, with Ilett's green.
Repeat, 12⁷/₈ x 9¹/₄ in. (32.7 x 23.5 cm)
Circ.251-1956.

148. Printed cotton furnishing; fern and flower stripes on spider's web ground. Printed by Samuel Matley & Son, Hodge, Cheshire, 1818.
Roller-printed.
Repeat, 12¹/₂ x 9¹/₈ in. (31.7 x 23.1 cm)
Circ.249-1956.

149. Printed cotton furnishing; vermicular pillars with flowers and feathers. About 1820.
Roller-printed in red on a yellow ground.
Repeat, 13³/₈ in. (34 cm) high, half-drop.
Circ.233-1956.

150. Printed cotton furnishing; floral trails on reserved areas in honeycomb ground. About 1820.
Roller-printed in red on a yellow ground.
Repeat, 11⁵/₈ x 12³/₈ in. (29.5 x 31.4 cm)
Circ.234-1956.

151. Printed cotton furnishing; scenes representing the British Isles. Probably printed by John Marshall & Sons, Manchester, about 1820.
Roller-printed in red.
Repeat, 21 in. (53.3 cm) high.
The Scottish and Welsh scenes were used in a French printed cotton of the 1820s.
T.43-956.

152-159. Designs for printed dress and shawl fabrics, some dated 1813 to 1824. Designed by the firm of Thomas Vaughan & Sons, London.
Watercolour on paper.

152. Floral stripe for printed shawl or dress with 'cashmere' design, dated "Jan. 4 1817" and marked "Done".
3 in. (7.6 cm) square.
E.1656-1913.

153. Designs for roller-printed cottons to be made by the Strines Printing Co., about 1824-25.
4¹/₄ x 7 in. (10.7 x 17.8 cm)
E.1655-1913.

154. Floral stripe, in the same style as plate 323 (dated 1817).
3¹/₄ x 2¹/₄ in. (8.3 x 5.7 cm)
E.1654-1913.

155. Motifs for roller-printing in a discharge, 1820s.
5¹/₄ x ³/₄ in. (13.3 x 1.9 cm)
E.1658-1913.

156. Designs for borders of printed shawls, or for printed cottons with 'cashmere' patterns. Inscribed with the names Price, Hargrave, Kebble, Spencer and Dugdale, along with "Francis, Norwich" (the latter being a shawl-weaving centre) and "Ed. Peele", for Edmund Peel of Church, where shawls were printed. Dated Nov. 1813 to Feb. 1814.
Overall, 7¹/₂ x 8¹/₂ in.(19 x 21.5 cm)
E.1659, 1660-1913.

157. Fern trails for a discharge print, 1820s.
5 x 1 in. (12.7 x 2.5 cm)
E.1657-1913.

158. Floral motifs for roller prints, 1820s.
3¹/₂ x 2 in. (8.9 x 5 cm)
E.1662-1913.

159. Trial sketches for delicate floral stripes, 1820s.
4¹/₂ x 8¹/₄ in. (11.4 x 21 cm)
E.1663-1913.

160. Design for a roller-print, dated 1824.
2 x 3¹/₂ in. (5 x 8.9 cm), mounted on side.
E.1661-1913.

161-172. Small pattern designs for printed dress materials. Drawn by Thomas Vaughan & Sons, London, 1820s. Watercolour on paper.
These designs were intended for roller-printing, the cylinders probably to be engraved by Lockett, whose strike-offs of 1826 and 1827 show patterns engraved for John Barge and for Thomas Barge, one of whom was presumably the Mr Barge named on designs plates 164 and 167.

161. Undulating stripes.
2¹/₈ x 2¹/₂ in. (5.3 x 6.4 cm)
E.1564-1913.

162. Floral stripes, marked 'DONE' on the back.
4¹/₄ x 7¹/₄ in. (10.8 x 18.4 cm)
E.1563-1913.

163. Floral undulating stripe, inscribed "Mr Maude".
2 x 2³/₈ in. (5 x 6 cm)
E.1562-1913.

164. Undulating stripe. Inscribed "Mr. Barge 1824", probably for John or Thomas Barge, calico printers at Broughton, Manchester.
2¹/₂ x 3¹/₂ in. (6.4 x 8.9 cm)
E.1566-1913.

165. Three small patterns for chintz; on the left marked 'not done', on the right marked 'done top'.
3⁷/₈ x 5¹/₂ in. (9.8 x 14 cm)
E.1568-1913.

166. Seaweed or fern pattern, marked 'not done'.
2¹/₂ x 3³/₄ in. (6.4 x 9.5 cm)
E.1565-1913.

167. Sketch in two colourways, inscribed "Mr Barge" (see plate 335).
3⁷/₈ x 3¹/₄ in. (9.8 x 8.2 cm)
E.1569-1913.

168. Sketches of unrelated motifs on a piece of paper addressed to "...Vaughan, Duke Str."
4³/₄ x 8¹/₄ in. (12 x 20.9 cm)
E.1571-1913.

169. Sketches for different motifs, inscribed "Mr Maude 1824".
4 x 3 in. (10.2 x 7.6 cm)
E.1567-1913.

170. Fern stems and stripes.
2³/₄ x 1¹/₄ in. (7 x 3.2 cm)
E.1572-1913.

171. Plant stripes (mounted on side).
7³/₄ x 1³/₄ in. (19.7 x 4.5 cm)
E.1573-1913.

172. Stripes crossed by plants in reserved areas.
1³/₄ x 2³/₄ in. (4.5 x 7 cm)
E.1570-1913.

173-184. Samples of printed cotton from a book of dye recipes used at Catterall, Lancashire, dated February 1824 to December 1824. The firm producing these printed cottons is likely to have been Henry Fielding Bros.
Block- and roller-printed.
Each, 2¹/₂ to 3 x 3 to 4 in. (6.3 to 7.6 x 7.6 to 10.2 cm)
T.12-1956.

173. Page 2. Flowers and tassels. Dated Feb. 13th 1824.Printed in 'paste red' and dyed in 'Strasburge Madder' and 'Shumac'.

174. Page 5. Spotted drapery. Dated Feb. 16th 1824. Printed in 'new Red' and dyed in 'French Madder' and 'disolved Glue'.

175. Page 110. Cube pattern. Dated Dec. 6th 1824. "Single Colours printed by Cylinder in paste red", dyed in French madder, Peachwood and Shumac.

176. Page 25. Rainbow style. Dated April 28th 1824. "Rainbow Style printed by the Block in 2 Reds and 2 Purples", dyed "in French Madder and nothing more"... "Boil in the Clearing paste for Covering with Croam yellow" (i.e. Chrome yellow). This and another piece marked "These were the First Rainbows done at Catteral".

177. Page 56. Rainbow style with floral trails. Dated September 12th 1824. "Rainbow... printed by Block in No. 2 Red and 16 purple for dyeing in Madder and Dipping (Pale Blue). And printing in Croam yellow".

178. Page 40. A discharge pattern. Dated June 12th 1824. "... printed in 40 acid and padded in No. 15 Lt. Chot. for Brown", Dyed with 'wolds', boiled off with "dutch madder.. Bark.. Shumac", "Grounding Berry yellow".

179. Page 34. Flower heads in the lapis style. May 30th, 1824. This sample was blotched in resist red for dipping blue and dyed with Dutch madder, then grounded in Berry yellow to give orange over the pink, green over the blue.

180-181. Page 100. Two samples stuck over a later recipe for clearing Turkey reds, dated March 7th 1825. At the right, a rainbow style with a pattern in chrome yellow. At the left, a similar effect achieved by padding in pale red and printing over by cylinder in gum red, the edge to the stripe being stippled. Pattern in chrome yellow.

182-184. Page 63. Small stars, clouds and fan shapes. Dated September 16th 1824. Dipped blue and madder make the rich coloured ground in the two lower samples.

185. Furnishing printed cotton; stripes of jasmine and leaves. Printed by Samuel Matley & Son, Hodge, Cheshire, 1824. Roller-printed in purple and yellow.
Repeat, 13³/₈ x 12¹/₂ in. (34 x 31.7 cm)
Circ.261-1956.

186. Furnishing printed cotton; stripes of roses and fern. Printed by Samuel Matley & Son, Hodge, Cheshire, 1824. Roller-printed in blue and yellow.
Repeat, 13³/₄ x 12 in. (35 x 30.5 cm)
Circ.259-1956.

187. Furnishing printed cotton; stripes of passion flower and lace. Printed by Samuel Matley & Son, Hodge, Cheshire, 1824. Roller-printed discharge.
Repeat, 13¹/₂ x 12¹/₂ in. (34.2 x 31.7 cm); sample smaller.
Circ.262-1956.

188. Furnishing printed cotton; flowers in curves of a leafy meander. Printed by Samuel Matley & Son, Hodge, Cheshire, 1824.
Roller-printed discharge on indigo ground, with additional colours by surface roller.
Repeat, 13¹/₂ x 12¹/₄ in. (34.2 x 31.2 cm)
Circ.267-1956.

189. Furnishing chintz; foxgloves. About 1825-30. Roller-printed in red, with other colours added by surface roller. Double green.
Repeat, 13¹/₈ in. (33.2 cm) high, half-drop.
T.70-1964.

190. Furnishing chintz; 'India shawl stripe' and 'needlework' flowers in bunches. Probably printed at Bannister Hall for Miles and Edwards, about 1825.
Block-printed .
Repeat, 12¹/₈ in. (31 cm) high, flower-bunch stripe in halfdrop repeat. The same medallions with a different alternate stripe appear in a Miles and Edwards sample book (T.209-1925, No. 741), also the tiny flowers to either side (No. 739), both first dated March 1825. A Bannister Hall pattern book shows samples in the same style, dated 1826, called an 'India shawl stripe'.
Circ.101-1960.

191. "Worm ground Needlework Chintz and Stripe". Printed at Bannister Hall for Clarkson and Turner, 1830-36.
Roller-printed with additional colours by surface roller or block.
Repeat, 14¹/₄ in. (36.1 cm) high, border; 11³/₄ in (29.8 cm) high, filling.
Bannister Hall samples 6528 and 6529 are of this pattern in a different colourway, sold from 1830 to 1836 by Clarkson and Turner. The 'worm ground' dates from 1830.
T.52-1911.

192. Furnishing chintz; floral stripes. About 1825.
Block-printed resist on a dipped blue ground.
Repeat, 12¹/₄ x 13 in. (31.2 x 33 cm)
T.166-1958.

193. Furnishing chintz; large pillars and flowers on a ground with small floral trails. About 1805.
Block-printed in madder colours with pencilled blue.
No blue threads.
Repeat, 14³/₄ in. (37.5 cm) high, half-drop.
T.157-1958.

194. Furnishing chintz; pillar with flowers. About 1830.
Roller-printed in black and red, with double green and other colours added by surface roller.
Repeat, 14¹/₄ in. (36.2 cm) high.
At the Henry Francis du Pont Winterthur Museum another colourway of this cotton has a single green. Despite the double green the colouring of plate 194 is radically different from that of plate 193.
T.308-1971.

195. Printed blind; view of a church seen through a pointed arch. About 1830-35.
Block-printed in the madder style with added blue and yellow.
Repeat, 16¹/₂ x 20 in. (42 x 50.8 cm) including half-drop. There are four scenes in the width of the material, and a fretwork pattern (here at the right) at each edge.
T.5-1933.

196. Furnishing chintz, possibly for a blind; Gothic windows. About 1830-35.
Roller-printed in red and black with blue and yellow added by surface roller.
Repeat, 12³/₈ x 17³/₈ in. (31.5 x 44.2 cm) including half-drop.
T.354-1972.

197. Furnishing chintz; vase with flowers, birds and fruits. 1830.
Roller-printed with fancy machine-ground. Double green.
Repeat, 14 in. (35.5 cm) high.
This is one of the earliest printed cottons copying birds from Audubon's *Birds of America* (plates. 8, 13), which came out as separate plates from 1827, but in the first complete volume in 1830. Plates 197 to 210 are unfaded samples from a dated but unnamed pattern book of a Lancashire cotton printing firm.
Circ.286-1956.

198. Furnishing chintz; naturalistic flowers over scrollwork stripes. 1830.
Roller-printed, with fancy machine-ground.
Additional colours by surface roller.
Repeat, 14³/₄ in. (37.5 cm) high, half-drop.
Circ.313-1956.

199. Printed cotton furnishing; stylized floral trails between all-over myriad florets. 1831.
Roller-printed .
Repeat, 13¹/₄ in .(33.7 cm) high, half-drop.
Circ.351-1956.

200. Printed cotton furnishing; stripes of acanthus scroll containing stars. 1831.
Roller-printed, with a single green.
Repeat, 13³/₈ x 12¹/₄ in. (34 x 31 cm)
Circ.350-1956.

201. Printed cotton furnishing; lace meanders
and flowers. 1831.
Roller-printed in purple and red with additional
colours by surface roller.
Repeat, 14³/₄ x 12¹/₄ in. (37.5 x 31 cm)
The pattern is reminiscent of brocaded silks of the 1760s and
plate-printed cottons of the 1760s to 1770s.
Circ.319-1956.

202. Printed cotton furnishing; naturalistic flowers
and grasses. 1831.
Roller-printed in red and purple, with blue, yellow and solid
green added by surface roller. The solid green is overprinted
with yellow in places to give a more natural colour.
Repeat, 14¹/₂ x 12 in. (37 x 30.5 cm)
Reminiscent of the naturalistic flower designs of the
later 18th century.
Circ.320-1956.

203. Printed cotton furnishing; birds and flowers. 1834.
Printed in two colours from stippled rollers, with additional
colours by surface roller. Single green overprinted yellow.
Repeat, 13¹/₄ in. (33.6 cm) high.
The birds are taken from Audubon's *Birds of America*, plates
20, 48, 53, 142, 152. The Victoria and Albert Museum has
seven colourways of this design.
Circ.305-1956.

204. Printed cotton furnishing; birds and pine cones;
leaves in stripes. 1830.
Roller-printed, with additional colours by surface roller.
Repeat, 14⁷/₈ x 12 in. (37.8 x 30.5 cm)
The birds are taken from Audubon's *Birds of America*, plates
25, 67. The Museum has seven colourways of this design.
Circ.277-1956.

205. Printed cotton furnishing; flowers and plaid ribbons,
with a gothic diaper ground. 1836.
Roller-printed in purple and red; blue, yellow and buff added
by surface roller, making double green and orange.
Repeat, 13 in. (33 cm) high, half-drop.
Circ.355-1956.

206. Printed cotton furnishing; naturalistic and heavily
stylised flowers on check ground. 1836.
Roller-printed in purples and reds; blue and yellow added by
surface roller, making double green and orange.
Repeat, 15¹/₂ x 12¹/₂ in. (39.4 x 31.7 cm)
Circ.356-1956.

207. Printed cotton furnishing; broken branches and
naturalistic flowers. 1837.
Roller-printed, with additional colours by surface roller.
Repeat, 13 x 12¹/₈ in. (33 x 30.8 cm)
Circ.370-1956.

208. Printed cotton furnishing; stripes of ribbon meander
and bunches of flowers. 1839.
Roller-printed in red and purple, with other colours
by surface roller.
Repeat, 13¹/₂ in. (34.2 cm) high, half-drop.
Circ.373-1956.

209. Printed cotton furnishing; flowers in silhouette on
zig-zag ground. 1846. Probably padded in pale red, printed
over by cylinder in gum red and finally printed in chrome
yellow, like the sample 181.
Repeat, 13³/₄ in. (34.9 cm) high, half-drop.
Circ.376-1956.

210. Printed cotton furnishing; fantastic flowers on
rainbow stripe. 1846.
Roller-printed in two shades of red; yellow and green
added by surface roller.
Repeat, 14 in. (35.5 cm) high, half-drop.
Circ.375-1956.

211. Printed cotton with border; 'cashmere' design. Printed for
Miles and Edwards, and later for Hindley & Sons, 1840s.
Roller-printed .
Repeat, 9²/₃ in. (24.5 cm) high, border; 1¹/₂ in. (3.8 cm), filling.
An identical filling is in a group of swatches (T.217-1925) with
the label of Miles and Edwards. The design is inspired by
woven and printed shawls of about 1815-25.
Circ.1060-1925.

212. Printed cotton with border; "cashmere design".
Printed for Miles and Edwards, 1840s.
Roller-printed, with a padded green ground.
Repeat, 15¹⁵/₁₆ in. (40.5 cm) high, border; 9³/₄ in. (24.6 cm)
This pattern is also in T.217-1925 with a Miles & Edwards
label. The design is inspired by woven and printed shawls of
the late 1830s .
Circ.1053-1925.

213-224. Samples of printed cottons for furnishing.
From three order books of Miles and Edwards, dated 1821-40.
Roller-and block-printed; the latter probably at Bannister Hall;
the former, some by John Lowe & Co, Shepley, some possibly
by Samuel Matley & Son, Hodge.
Each sample, about 3 x 4 in. (7.6 x 10.2 cm).

213. Leopard spots on diagonal stripe ground. Printed at
Bannister Hall. Sales noted April 1821 to November 1826.
Another leopard spot design sold by Miles and Edwards in
1821 matches a sample in a Bannister Hall design patent
book of 1802. This design may also date from the first
decade and, like other leopard spots, have retained its
popularity through the 1830s.
T.209-1925, No. 47.

214. Broad stripe with fancy edging.
Sales noted April 1825 to July 1830. A colourway in blue
and white was sold between 1826 and 1835.
T.209-1925, No. 779.

215. 'Wood-grain' stripe with fancy edge.
This pattern appears in seven colourways in the Miles and
Edwards books, from No. 868 (February 1826) to No. 1170
(October 1827), selling until at least 1830. The same pattern
occurs, dated November and December 1825, in a transit
book containing samples printed by Samuel Matley &
Son, Hodge.
T.210-1925, No.928.

216. Rosette on fancy net stripe ground.
Sales noted between December 1826 and March 1827. The
same rosette on a plain diagonal 'buff line' ground (as in
plate 213) was sold by Miles and Edwards in 1821 (No. 73)
and may be a still earlier design.
T.210-1925, No. 980.

217. Gothic stripe.
Sold in this colourway May 1827 to January 1830. Printed
by John Lowe of Shepley Hall, Lancashire, from a roller
engraved by Lockett, March 14th 1827. Miles and Edwards
sold a version in two reds with a tea-ground from April
1827 to at least December 1830.
T.210-1925, No. 1079.

218. Stippled floral stripe.
Sales in this colourway noted from June 1827 to July 1830.
Sold in nine different colourways, the first appearing in
March 1827 (No. 1027).
T.210-1925, No. 1098.

219. Floral 'damask' in two yellows.
Sales noted June 1827 to November 1829. Ackermann's
Respository of January 1809 noted a new prevailing style
with only two shades of one colour used in printed cottons
'to produce the appearance of damask'. A pattern from a
17th century woven silk was printed in two reds at
Bannister Hall in 1807 and was still being sold by Miles
and Edwards from 1821 to 1827.
T.210-1925, No. 1100.

220. 'Watered' stripe.
Sales noted in this colourway from May 1828 to June
1833. Like the 'damask' of plate 219 or the 'twill' effect in
plate 213, this is another imitation of a woven silk in a
printed cotton.
T.210-1925, No. 1302.

221. Floral diaper.
Sales noted from December 1837 to September 1844 and
'carried' into a later, missing, book. Other colourways in
two reds, in green and cream, in terracotta red and yellow.
T.211-1925, No. 5106.

222. Gothic trellis, with heraldic rose.
Sales noted January 1838 to January 1839.
T.211-1925, No. 5228.

223. Urns and flowers in diamond shapes with striped and checkered grounds.
Sales noted from December 1838 to January 1843, with reference to a number (in an earlier, missing, book) which would be of about 1830. Another version with plain blue and buff grounds sold until 1844. This design may have been taken directly from a woven silk, for a garment from the Aegean Islands with a silk in this pattern exists in the Victoria and Albert Museum (4142-1856) .
T.211-1925, No. 5438.

224. Hieroglyphs in stripes. Sales noted from 1838 to 1840. This and another colourway existed in the book of 1830-37, now missing.
T.211-1925, No. 5456.

225-231. Seven swatches of printed cotton furnishings with lattice and strapwork patterns. Probably printed at Bannister Hall. Sold by Miles and Edwards in the 1830s.
Roller-printed, with optional fancy machine-grounds.

225. Elaborate pattern in red and black on a fancy machine-ground.
Repeat, $9^5/_{16}$ x $8^3/_4$ in. (23.7 x 22.2 cm)
Circ.1088-1925.

226-227. Two colourways of a rope lattice pattern, about 1837. Repeat, $3^5/_8$ x $2^1/_8$ in. (9.2 x 5.4 cm)
Circ.1108-1925, Circ.1105-1925.

228. Strapwork in two colours on a fancy machine-ground.
Repeat, $4^3/_4$ x $4^3/_8$ in. (12 x 11.1 cm)
Probably designed by Thomas Willement, judging from the similarity to plate 230
Circ.1095-1925.

229. Narrow network with a wider network pattern superimposed.
Repeat, $5^1/_4$ x $3^1/_8$ in. (13.3 x 8 cm)
Circ.1098-1925.

230. "Elizabethan"; strapwork pattern.
Designed by Thomas Willement in the early 1830s, probably as a wallpaper. Printed cottons in two pattern sizes and a worsted damask were also made from the design. The wallpaper and a printed cotton survive at Charlecote Park, Warwickshire. The Miles and Edwards order books show a worsted damask on sale from 1834, and printed cottons from December 1837 to 1844, the earlier and later sales books being missing.
Repeat in the size shown here, $9^3/_8$ x $6^{11}/_{16}$ in. (23.8 x 17 cm)
Circ.1106-1925.

231 Fretwork pattern on a "Polygon" fancy machine-ground.
Repeat, $5^3/_8$ x $3^1/_4$ in. (13.7 x 8.2 cm)
A popular design printed in several colourways in 1838-39 and sold until at least 1844. The 'polygon' ground is named in a sample dated March 1837 in a Bannister Hall pattern book.
T.111-1925 contains a sample (5318) of fretwork pattern on polygon ground dated June 1838.
Circ.1103-1925 .

232. Printed cotton for furnishing; flowers on an elaborate fancy-ground. 1840s.
Roller-printed .
Repeat, $18^1/_2$ in. (47 cm) high, half-drop.
T.414-1967.

233. Printed cotton furnishing; flowers in rococo cartouches. 1840s.
Roller-printed.
Repeat, 18 in. (45.7 cm) high.
T.410-1967.

234. Printed cotton furnishing; floral trails on a shaded stripe ground. 1840s.
Roller-printed.
Repeat, about 18 in. (45.7 cm) high.
T.407-1967.

235. Corner of a printed shawl; adorsed, angled pines in an arcade, with inner border (gallery) and cornerpiece. Printed by Charles Swaisland of Crayford, Kent, who registered the three designs of border, gallery and cornerpiece in December 1845. The copyright obtained by this registration lasted only until September 1846.
Block-printed wool.
Shawl, approximnately 66in (167.6cm) square. Border and gallery 19^1/$_2$ in. (49.5 cm) high.
T.203-1978.

236. Printed shawl; symmetrically placed pines, intermingled with asymmetrical foliage, with no repeat in the half of the shawl shown. Printed by Charles Swaisland, Crayford, Kent; 1850. The design of this shawl, found on paper in the archive of G. P. & J. Baker, is undated, but has the Swaisland reference numbers H.1541, H.1542, H.1543 (for field, border and endpieces). Other designs numbered H.1528 and H.1589 are dated respectively August and October 1850. This elaborate design, which may have taken over five hundred blocks to print, is characterised by exotic stylised vegetation with fern-like leaves found in many designs for woven and printed shawls around the time of the Great Exhibition of 1851.
Block-printed wool.
Shawl, approximately 140 x 72 in. (355.6 x 182.88 cm).
T.334-1987.

2: Block-impression on paper imitating Chinese painted silk. Dated 1748,
E.141-1964

3: Design for block-print, by John Baptist Jackson, about 1745-55. E.4487-1920

5: Design for block-print by John Baptist Jackson, about 1745-55. E.4529-1920

6-7: Block-impression on paper (in two parts), designed by John Baptist
Jackson, 1745-55. E.4533, E.4538-1920

8: Furnishing chintz; probably designed by John Baptist Jackson, c.1750.
T.243-1979

9-10: Plate-printed cotton by Robert Jones & Co, Old Ford, 1761. Printed from two copper-plates. 442-1897

11. Paper impression of a printed textile. Bromley Hall, Middlesex, about 1765. E.458(210, 211)-1955

12-13: Plate-printed linen and cotton (2 copper-plates) with additional block-printed colours, Robert Jones & Co, Old Ford, 1769. T.140-1934

14. Paper-impression from the Bromley Hall pattern book, imitation of
embroidery, 1760s -1770s. E.458(38)-1955

15 Plate-printed cotton, rococo design in china blue, Bromley Hall,
1760s-1770s. T.137-1956

16: Design for block-print, based on silk design. Late 1740s or early 1750s. 7275.106

17: Design imitating embroidery. 1750s or 1760s. 7275.39

19: Design for block-printed textile. 1760s or 1770s. 7275.40

52

20

7275. 338.

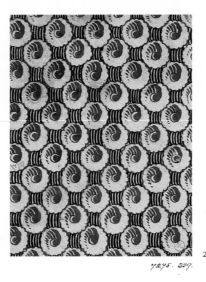

21

7275. 339.

22

7275. 340.

23

7275. 341.

20-23: Designs for printed dress fabrics, 1760s or 1770s. 20: 7275.340; 21
7275.339; 22: 7275.338; Plate 23 inscribed 'Peele & Simpson', 7275.338-341

25: Design for block-printed textile, 1760s.
7275.204

54

26: Patchwork of printed and painted cottons, some Indian. Part of a set of bed hangings made in the third quarter of the 18th century. T.242-1908

28. Paper-impression of a printed textile design. Bromley Hall, Middlesex, late
1760s or early 1770s. E.458(74, 75)-1955

58

29. Paper-impression of a printed textile design. Bromley Hall, Middlesex,
1170s or early 1780s. E.458(20, 21)-1955

30. Paper-impression of a printed textile design. Bromley Hall, Middlesex,
1770s or early 1780s. E.458(22, 23)-1955

61

31. Paper-impression of a printed textile design. Bromley Hall, Middlesex,
1770s. E.458(68, 69)-1955

62

32. Design for textile, for printing by John Munns,
Crayford, Kent, 1760s or 1770s. 7275.297

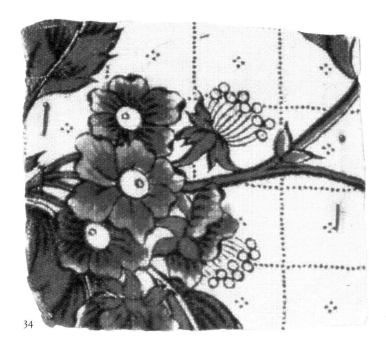

64

34

35

36

37

38

39

34-39: Printed dress fabrics dated 1752, 1760, 1766, 1779, 1780, 1781, from the pages of Barbara Johnson's Album. T.219-1973

40: Plate-printed fustian "Lethe, or Aesop in the Shades".
Between 1766 and 1764. T.75-1914

66

41

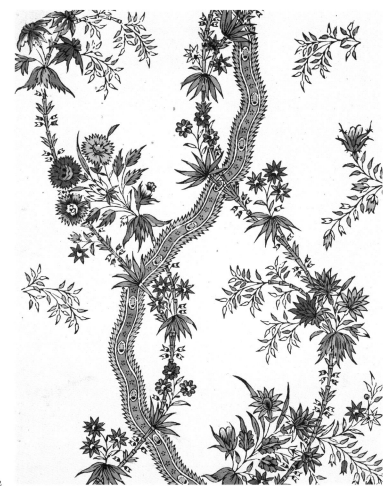

42

43

44

41-44: Four block-impressions, colourways of one pattern showing variations in treatment, 1770s-1780s. 41: E.1863-1921; 42: E.1562-1921; 43: E.1372-1921; 44: E.1710-1921

45: Block-impression on paper, 1770s or 1780s. E.1403-1921

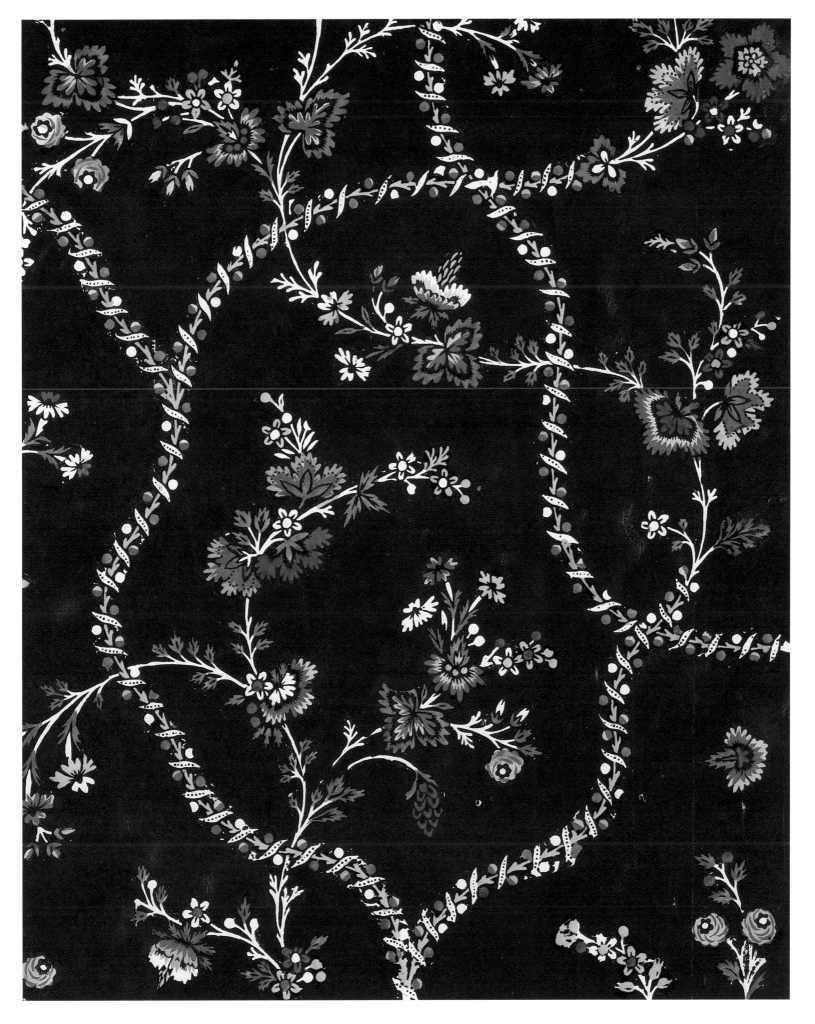

47: Block-impression on paper, 1770s or 1780s. E.1689-1921

70

49: Printed dress material. About 1780.
T.94-1912

51: Detail from printed cotton dress, c.1780.
T100-1966

52

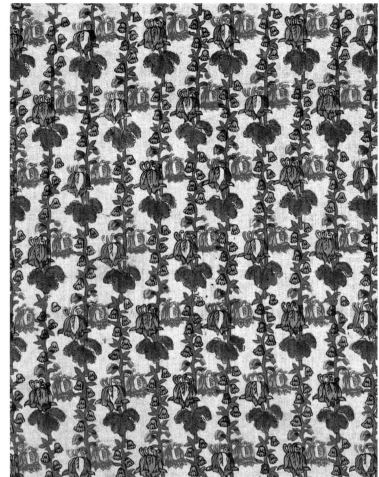

53

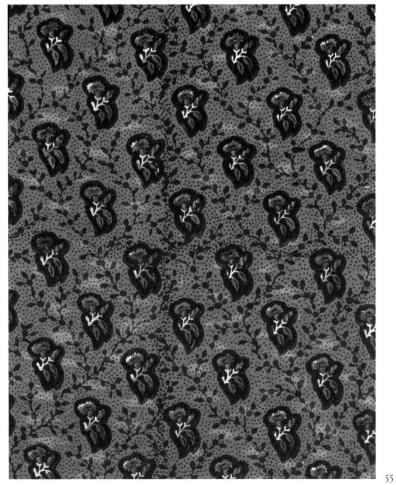

54

55

52-55: Details from printed cotton dresses. 52: c.1785, T.274-1967; 53: c.1790, T.286-1968; 54: 1780s, T.296-1973; 55: 1785-95, T.99-1966

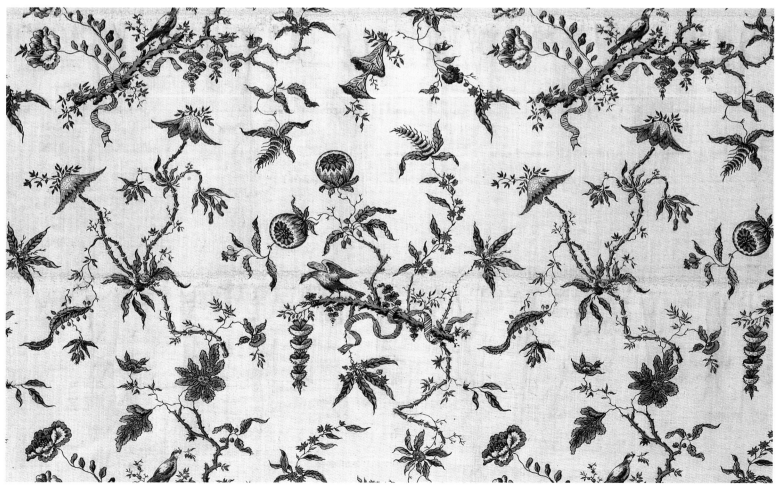

57: Printed cotton, fantastic flowers, birds and ribbons in the manner of
Pillement. About 1775-85. Circ.363-1955

58: Block impression on paper for border of printed cover or kerchief,
matching plate 60, 1770s or 1780s. E.1379-1921

59-63: Five block-impressions, 1770s or 1780s. 59, 60, 61, 62 for dress fabrics or handkerchiefs, E.1375, E.1378, E.1376, E.1377-1921. 63: Quarter of medalion for cover or kerchief, E.1374-1921

64: Plate-printed cotton designed by David Richards, c.1780.
Circ.90-196065: Plate-printed cotton, dated 1790. T.50-1933

65: Plate-printed cotton, dated 1790. T.50-1933

66: Paper-impression of a printed textile design. Bromley Hall, Middlesex, late
1770s into the 1780s. E.458(147, 148)-1955

67: Printed cotton. Bromley Hall, Middlesex, about 1775. Circ.91-1960

68: Design for printed textile, William Kilburn,
c.1790. E.894-1978, p.149a

69: Design for printed textile, William Kilburn, c.1790. E.894-1978, p.41

70: Design by William Kilburn for a printed textile, c.1790. E.894-1978, p.17

84

71: Design for a printed textile, William Kilburn, c.1790. E.894-1978, p.19

72: Design by William Kilburn for a furnishing chintz, 1792. E.894-1978, p.73

73. Design by William Kilburn for a furnishing chintz, c.1792. E.894-1978, p.75

74: Design by William Kilburn for a chintz border, c.1792. E.894-1978, p.71

88

76: Design for printed textile, William Kilburn, c.1787-92.
E.894-1978, p.110(a)

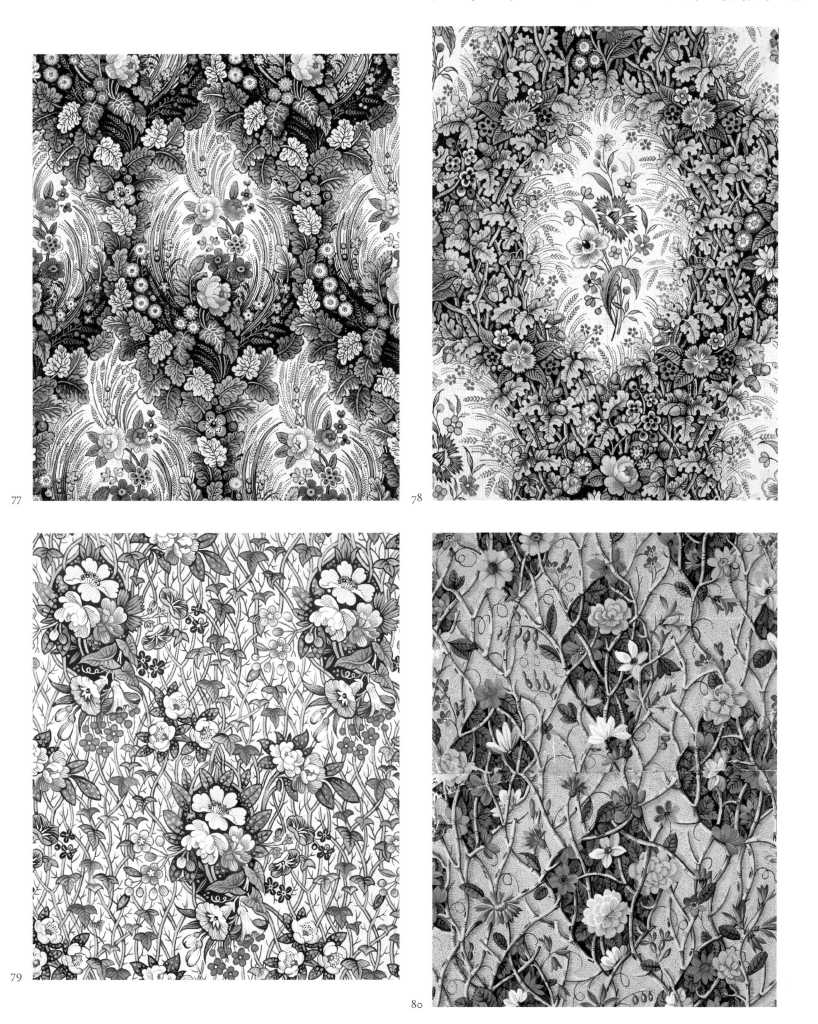

89

77

78

79

80

79: Design for a printed textile by William Kilburn, 1791. E.894-1978 p.92(a)
80: Design for printed textile by William Kilburn, c.1791. E.894-1978, p.110(b)

90

82: Design for printed textile by William Kilburn, 1791.
E.894-1978, p.58(a)

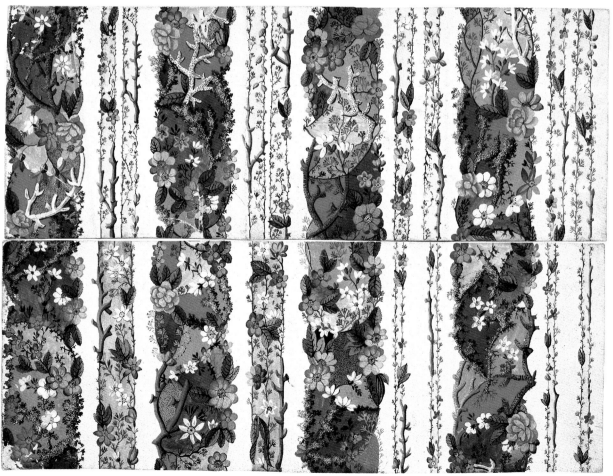

84: Design for printed textile by William Kilburn, c.1791-2.
E.894-1978, p.57(b)

92

86: Block-printed cotton. About 1785-95.
T.37-1965

87: Block-printed cotton possibly designed by John Edwards.
About 1790. T.64-1955

94

88: Paper-impression of a printed textile. Merton Abbey, about 1780-83 and
later at Bromley Hall. E.458(26)-1955

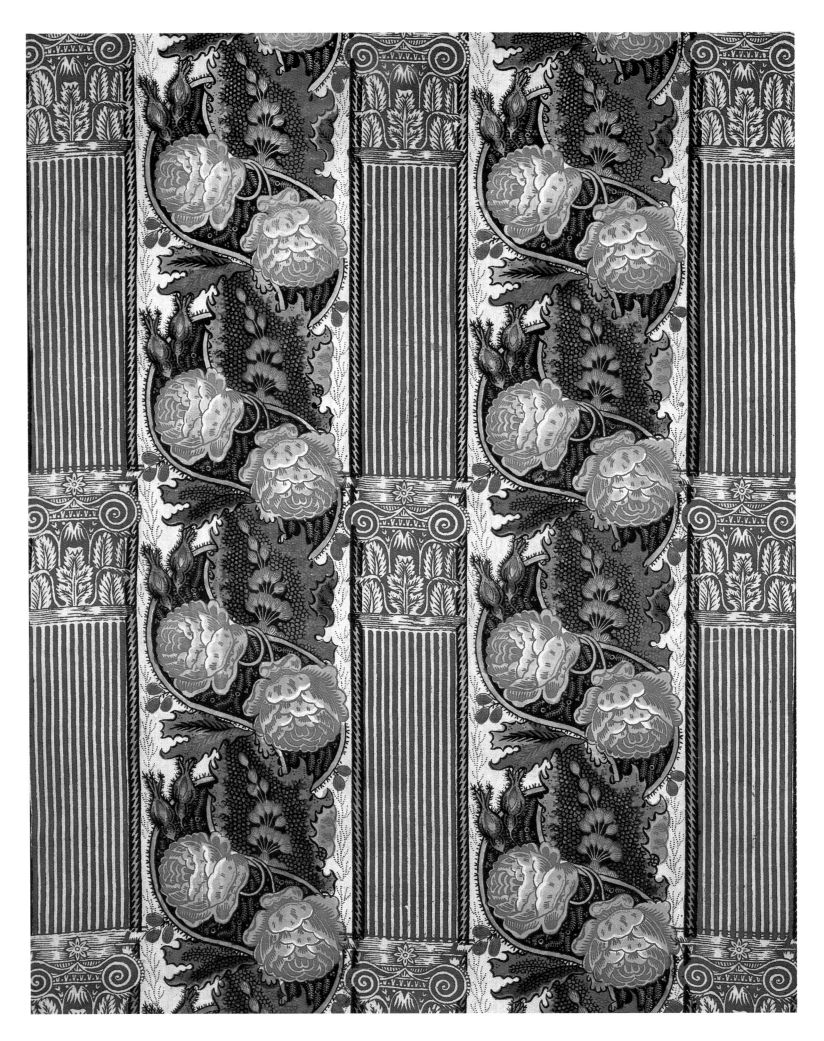

90: Block-printed furnishing chintz. Pillar-print. About 1790. T.2-1958

92: Furnishing chintz printed at Fordingbridge,
Hampshire, c.1790. T.115-1927

93: Block-printed furnishing chintz. About 1790. Circ.100-1960

94: Block-printed furnishing chintz. About 1790-95. T.428-1976

100

95: Patchwork quilt of printed cottons. Dated 1797. T.102-1938

97: Detail of patchwork. T.102-1938

98-106: Printed dress fabrics, dated from 1789 to 1812, from the pages of
Barbara Johnson's Album. T.219-1973

107: Block printed furnishing chintz
probably designed by John Edwards.
About 1795. T.25-1930

109: Furnishing chintz, c.1800.
Circ.493a-1956

104

110: "Royal Oak & Ivy", furnishing, block-printed at Bannister Hall for Richard Ovey, 1799. Circ.86-1960

III: "Scarlet Ground White Passion Flower Chintz", printed at Bannister Hall
for Richard Ovey, 1802. Circ.334-1955

112: Detail of a curtain in Pompeian colours, c.1804-10. T.138-1973

113

114

109

115

113-115: Borders printed for E.B. Dudding, c.1804. T.86-1964, samples
numbered: neoclassical 151; Egyptian 239, 240

116

117

118

116-118: Borders block-printed for E.B. Dudding, c.1802-14. T.86-1964,
samples numbered: 64,66, 417

119

120

121

119-123: Borders block-printed for E.B. Dudding, c.1802-14, T.86-1964.
Samples numbered: neoclassical, 116, 117; gothic, 118, floral, 6

122

123

112

125: "The One Stripe Needlework Flower Pot Chintz Border", 1805.
Printed at Bannister Hall for Richard Ovey. T.42-1925

127: Furnishing chintz. Printed at Bannister Hall for Richard Ovey, 1802. Circ.495-1956

114

129: Pillar-print, 'demy' chintz in drab style,
c.1805. Circ.223-1956

131: 'Demy' chintz in drab style, c.1805.
Circ.221-1956

116

133: Discharge-printed cotton furnishing.
About 1805. Circ.230-1956

134: Discharge-printed cotton, c.1805. Circ.227-1956

118

135

136

137

137: 'Lapis style' print, about 1808-15. Circ.243-1956

138: Furnishing chintz by Peel & Co., Church, 1812. Circ.268-1955

120

141: Printed cotton with dipped blue ground, Samuel Matley & Son, Cheshire, 1816. Circ.267-1955

142: Block-printed furnishing chintz,
c.1815. T.394-1966

143: Furnishing chintz, c.1815.
Circ.352b-1955

144: Printed centre for a quilt or cover,
c.1815. Circ.606-1956

145-146: Roller-printed cottons with single green, Samuel Matley & Son,
Hodge, Cheshire, 1818. Circ.248-1956, Circ.247-1956

147-148: Roller-printed cottons. Samuel Matley & Son, Hodge, Cheshire, 1818.
Circ.251-1956, Circ.249-1956

149-150: Roller-printed cottons, c. 1820. Circ.233-1956, Circ.234-1956

151: Roller-printed cotton furnishing. Scenes representing the
British Isles. Probably printed by John Marshall & Sons Ltd, Manchester.
About 1820. T.43-1956

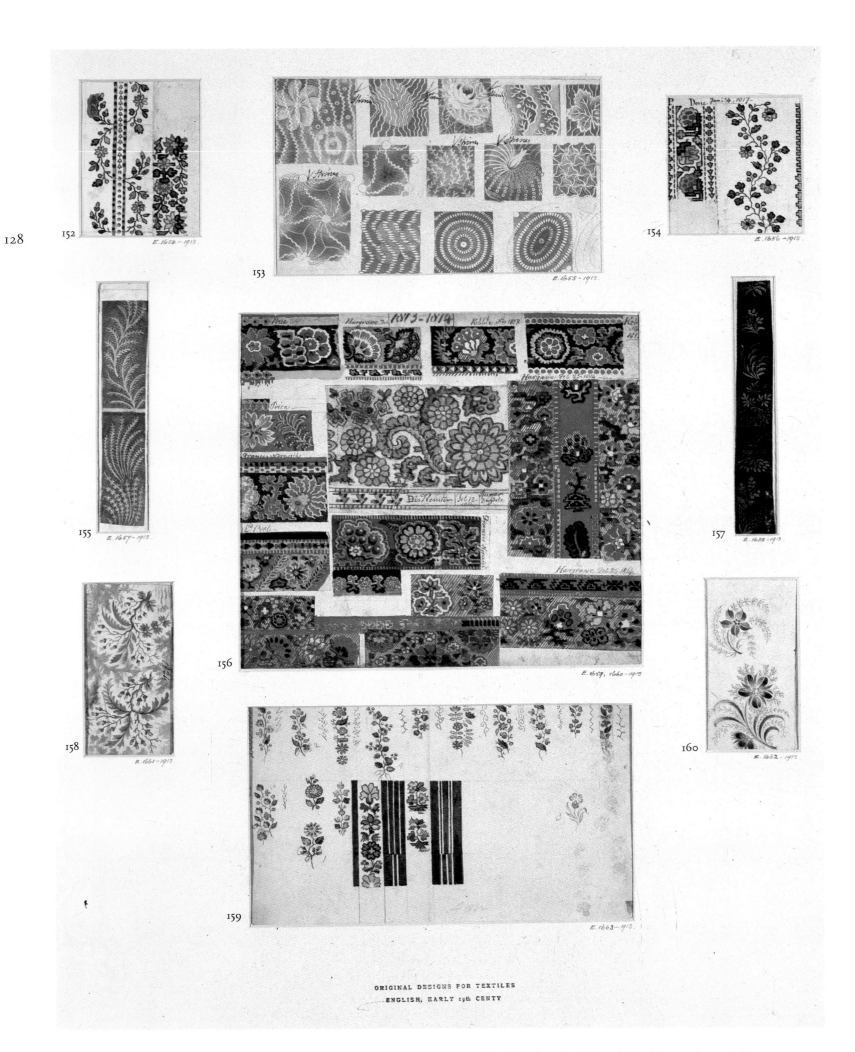

128

152   E.1654-1913.

153   E.1655-1913.

154   E.1656-1913.

155   E.1657-1913.

156   E.1659, 1660-1913.

157   E.1658-1913.

158   E.1661-1913.

160   E.1662-1913.

159   E.1663-1913.

ORIGINAL DESIGNS FOR TEXTILES
ENGLISH, EARLY 19th CENTY

152-160: Designs for printed dress & shawl fabrics. Drawn by Thomas Vaughan & Sons, London. Dated on various designs from 1813-1824

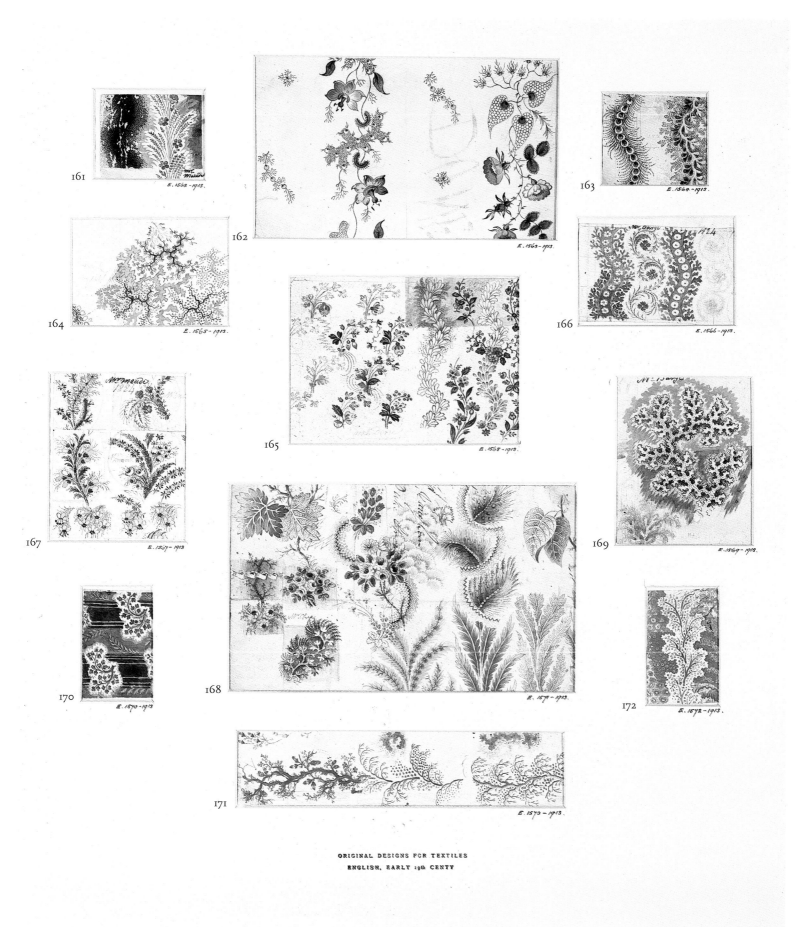

ORIGINAL DESIGNS FOR TEXTILES
ENGLISH, EARLY 19th CENTY

161-172: Designs by Thomas Vaughan & Sons for printed dress fabrics. Some dated
1824. E.1562-1913, E.1563-1913, E.1564-1913, E.1565-1913, E.1568-1913, E.1566-1913,
E.1567-1913, E.1571-1913, E.1569-1913, E.1570-1913, E.1573-1913, E.1572-1913

130

173-184: Samples of printed cotton from a book of dye recipes used at Catterall,
Lancashire, 1824-5. T.12-1956

185-186: Roller-printed furnishing cottons. Samuel Matley & Son, Hodge, Cheshire, 1824. Circ.261-1956, Circ.259-1956

187-188: Roller-printed discharge furnishing cottons. Samuel Matley & Son, Hodge, Cheshire, 1824. Circ. 262-1956, Circ.267-1956

189: Roller-printed furnishing cotton, c.1825-30. T.70-1964

134

191: Furnishing chintz with stylised flowers imitating embroidery. Probably printed at Bannister Hall, 1830-6. T.52-1911

192: Furnishing chintz. Block-printed resist on a dipped
blue ground, c. 1825. T.166-1958

137

195: Printed window blind, c.1830-35. T.5-1933

196: Furnishing chintz. Possibly for a window blind, c.1830-5. T.354-1972

197-198: Roller-printed furnishing chintzes, 1830. Circ.286-1956, Circ.313-1956

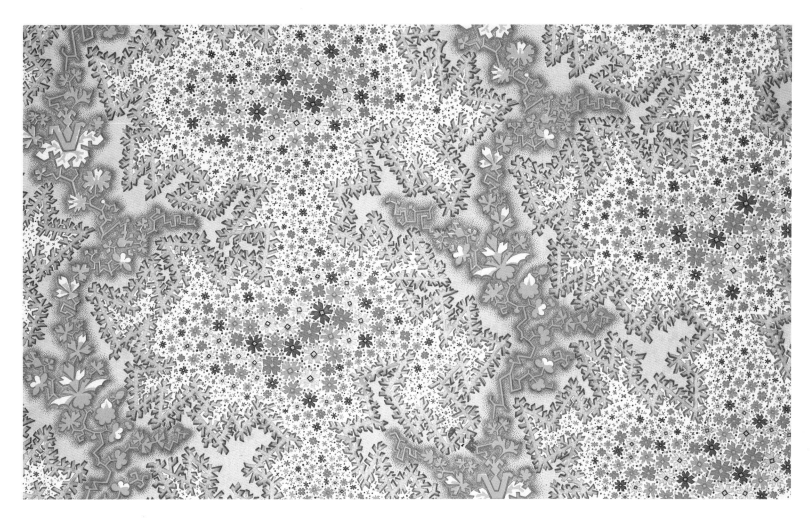

199-200: Cotton furnishings roller-printed in new colour combinations, 1831.
Circ.351-1956, Circ.350-1956

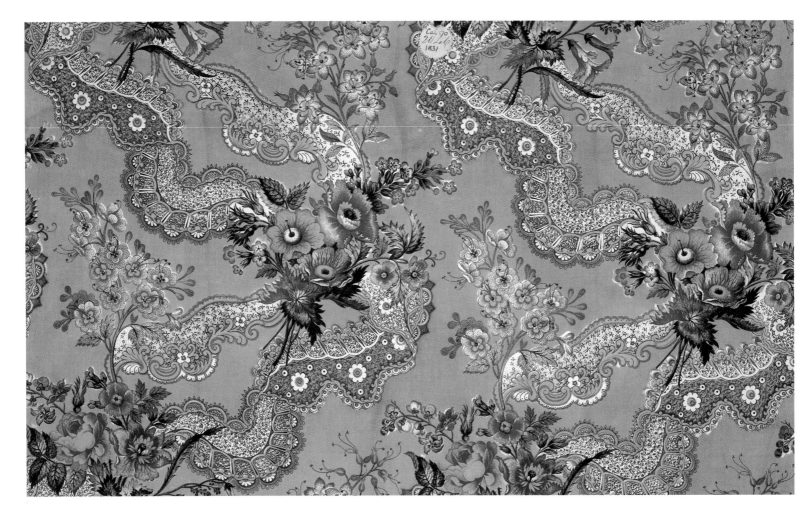

201-202: Roller-printed cottons, 1831. Circ. 319-1956, Circ.320-1956

203-204: Printed cotton furnishings with birds from Audubon's *Birds of America*, 204: 1834, Circ. 305-1956; 205: Circ.277-1956

205-206: Furnishing chintzes, 1836. Circ.355-1956, Circ.356-1956

208: Printed cotton furnishing, 1839.
Circ.373-1956

209-210: Printed cotton furnishings, 1846. Circ.376-1956, Circ.375-1956

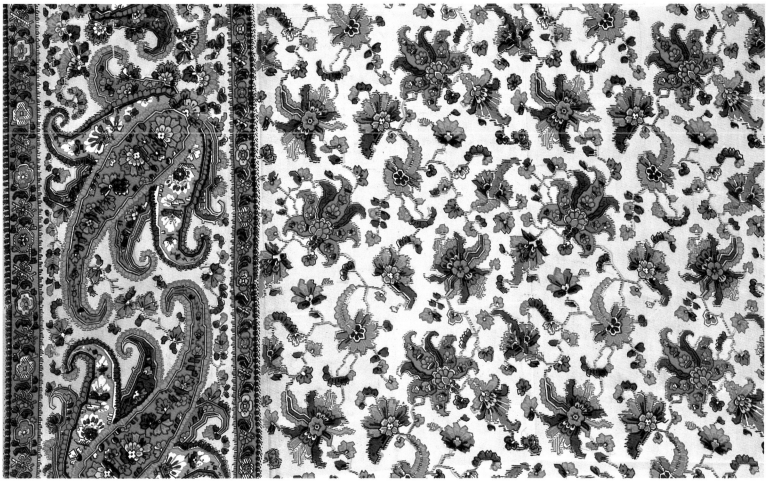

211-212: Printed cottons with designs of field and border derived from shawls, 1840s. Circ.1060-1925, Circ.1053-1925

148

213-224: Samples of printed cotton furnishings from order books of Miles and Edwards, dated 1821-1840. T.209,210,211-1925

225-231: Printed cottons, 1830s. Circ.1088-1925, Circ.1108-1925, Circ.1105-1925, Circ.1095-1925, Circ.1098-1925, Circ.1106-1925, Circ.1103-1925

150

232

233

234

232-234: Printed cotton furnishings, 1840s. T.414-1967; T.410-1967; T.407-1967

235. Corner of a shawl. Block-printed wool. Charles Swaisland,
Crayford, Kent. T.203-1978

236. Half a shawl. Block-printed wool. Charles Swaisland,
Crayford, Kent, 1850. T.334-1987

Glossary

BERRY YELLOW   Sometimes called 'Persian' or 'French' berries, fruit of the *Rhamnus Infectorius*, giving bright, rich yellows or drabs, according to the mordant used.

BLOCK PRINTING   Each colour, except those to be 'pencilled' (q.v.) was applied with a separate block of wood carved to leave the pattern for that particular colour in relief. Registration of the design was regulated by 'pins' at the corners. The printer grasped a shaped hand-hold or leather strap at the back of the block, pressed its face to a taut cloth saturated with dye or mordant that his assistant had prepared above a tub of the substance to be printed, then positioned the block by means of the pins and struck it with a mallet to make a smooth transfer of the printed matter. If finer details than could be carved in wood were required, metal strips and pins were inserted in the block.

BLUE THREADS   By the Act of 1774 all-cotton cloth could legally be sold and printed for use in Britain, but three blue threads had to be woven in the selvedges of cotton of English manufacture to identify it for payment of duty. This condition was dropped in 1811.

CHINA BLUE   An English invention, called 'bleu d'Angleterre' in France, this fine indigo blue technique overcame the problem of indigo oxidising and becoming insoluble on the way from dye vat to cloth. By printing the indigo as a paste with iron sulphate and a suitable thickener (such as gum arabic), the desired shade of blue could be obtained by dipping the cloth alternately in baths of lime and iron sulphate. As this technique could not be used with the many processes necessary for producing all the other chintz colours, the technique tended to be favoured for plate-prints, though the sample of Barbara Johnson's linen dress fabric in two shades of china blue (plate 1) shows how effective the monochrome block prints could be.

CHROME YELLOW   Chromate of lead. The first of the chrome dyes was invented in 1819 by Koechlin of Mulhouse. Chrome orange and green followed. John Mercer produced a chrome yellow in England in about 1823.

CLOUDS   In England, the name given to a textile with a pattern printed on the warp, or on warp and weft, before weaving, so producing imprecise outlines.

CYLINDER-PRINTING   Thomas Bell is credited with the invention in 1783. The cylinders used in Britain were at first of copper-plate hammered to shape and joined by brazing: as these joins tended to open, later cylinders were bored from solid metal. As broad as the cloth to be printed, the early cylinders were restricted in circumference, not being large enough for pictorial furnishing prints until about 1815. In spite of this, the new technique, so much faster than printing by hand, led to a strike by journeymen printers as early as 1790, and Livesey, Hargreaves, Anstie, Smith and Hall, who according to O'Brien had had some 600 or 700 cylinders cut and pinned, were threatened with arson in 1786 if they did not stop working their "Machines for Printing". O'Brien wrote of the possibility of printing by machine in four colours in 1790; and Bell had taken out a patent in 1784 for printing in five colours at once.

DEMY CHINTZ   In the mid-eighteenth century the 'half chintz' was composed of red, blue and yellow, which could be overprinted to produce other colours, but lacked the extra reds and purples of the 'whole chintz'. By the early nineteenth century the term 'demy' or 'demi-chintz' had a more restricted range, fewer than five colours, and was often used to denote the 'drab' style, with no reds.

DISCHARGE   Dischargers were not widely used until the early 19th century, though they were being advertised in the late 1780s. Printed on the cloth after dyeing or after mordanting, they made the colour either colourless or soluble so that it could be washed out, leaving a white figure to receive other colours.

FANCY MACHINE-GROUND   The elaboration of roller-prints in the 1820s and 1830s led to increasing use of fancy ground covers as alternatives to plain or coloured grounds. Those engraved by the firm of Joseph Lockett were particularly intricate.

FUSTIAN This name was used for several different fabrics, sometimes a twilled cotton or cotton and linen, sometimes with a nap. When printed, fustian was usually a plain weave cotton weft on linen warp, legal for printing in Britain from 1736 to 1774, when all-cotton cloth was banned in deference to the silk and woollen industries. Some dyes took differently on cotton and linen, producing a speckled effect..

LAPIS STYLE Before the invention of 'resist-red' the different processes for printing red and blue necessitated a white or black outline between the two colours. A resist for the blue dye, which at the same time contained a mordant for madder, made precise juxtaposition possible from 1808. The style was developed at Mulhouse and by James Thomson at Primrose, Lancashire.

MADDER COLOURS Pinks, reds, purples, brown and black could be dyed from madder by using different mordants.

MANGANESE BRONZE Hydrated peroxide of manganese. First produced at Mulhouse in 1815, the style was developed in England by John Mercer (see Biographies and Notes on firms).

MORDANT A substance which bonds certain dyes to cloth so that they cannot be washed out. Cloth printed with different mordants - such as iron, tin, alum - would emerge in shades of brown, black, red and purple from one dye bath. Iron, used for blacks and browns, tended to eat away the cloth.

PEACHWOOD Akin to Brazilwood, producing red, black and violet with various mordants, but of a fugitive nature.

PENCILLING In the early eighteenth century it was impossible to print indigo because of problems with oxidisation. It was discovered however, that dye held in the bristles of a paint brush could be protected from the air long enough to be painted or 'pencilled' onto the cloth, producing uneven and not always fast blue. Weld, to make green with the blue, was sometimes also pencilled rather than mordanted, and then was not fast.

PLATE-PRINTING Copper plates up to 36 inches square, with finely engraved designs, were used for printing monochrome pictorial designs in the second half of the eighteenth century, after the invention in Ireland in 1752 of thickeners suitable for printing dyes and mordants. Handkerchiefs and other items printed earlier from copper plates were in ordinary printers' ink that could not be washed. After roller-printing became common in the early nineteenth century, copper plates were used only for handkerchiefs.

QUERCITRON Bark of the yellow oak, native to North America. When mordanted, it made yellow with alum, drab with iron, olive with a mixture of the two. An American chemist, Edward Bancroft, patented its use in October 1775, and printers must have used it under licence from him. In 1779 a sale of printworks in Surrey advertised "a large Quantity of American yellow bark which, if not superior, is an excellent Substitute for Wold" (weld). When patent restrictions were lifted at the end of the 18th century, the general use of quercitron helped to promote the drab style.

RAINBOW STYLE Invented by the paper-stainer Spoerlin of Vienna and developed at Mulhouse, this was at first a block-printed style which was adapted for roller-printing. The principle was to provide different colours from parallel troughs to be merged by brush or roller at the edges after application to the cloth.

ROLLER-PRINTING See Cylinder-printing, surface Roller and Fancy machine-ground.

SHEPERTEE'S Name given to a garment with printed pattern (plate 34) in Barbara Johnson's Album. Madeleine Ginsburg suggested the word derived from 'shepherdess', possibly a fashionable form of jacket based on a rural garment.

SHUMAC (Sumac) An astringent agent assisting the dyeing process like a mordant, and also adding a yellowish tone.

STEAM COLOURS See Topical Colours

SURFACE ROLLER   Wooden rollers, cut in the same way as wood blocks, were used for areas of solid colour to supplement the fine engraved lines produced by the metal rollers. A 'union' or 'mule' machine to combine the two kinds of roller was invented about 1805 by James Burton of Church, Lancashire.

TEA-GROUND   A pale, weak brown colour much favoured for the grounds of colourful chintzes between 1805 and 1825, after which it was less popular than the finely engraved fancy grounds.

TOPICAL COLOURS   Colours printed in the form of thickened solutions, mixed with a mordant if necessary. This was a 19th century process for a mass market and was impermanent unless fixed by steaming, hence 'steam colours' which were comparatively fast. When not fixed the topical colours were sometimes called 'fancy' or 'spirit' colours.

TURKEY RED   A fine, bright red based on madder, first dyed on cotton cloth by Koechlin of Mulhouse in 1810. The style was very popular with discharge work for handkerchiefs and for export goods. There was a very large Turkey red industry in Scotland.

ADAMS, LAY & ADAMS   Were printing at Old Ford in 1772. Richard Adams and Samuel Lay of Old Ford were bankrupted in March 1786.

AMYAND, GEORGE   See Nixon, Francis.

BANNISTER HALL   A printworks from about 1798 to 1893, it was famous for block-printed "rich chintz Furnitures". Richard Jackson and John Stevenson were the original partners, joined in 1804 by John Swainson. Charles Swainson, with varying partners, ran the firm from 1809 to 1825. From 1825 to 1856 it was known as Charles Swainson & Co., then until 1893 Thomas Clarkson & Co. Important records from this printworks survive for the years 1799 to 1840.

BARGE   There were several printers of this name. (i) William Barge printed handkerchiefs at Bridgewater Street, Salford, from 1814; his widow and son carrying on the business until 1834. (ii) John Barge, with a partner named Foster until 1810, was printing at Broughton Bridge, Manchester, 1806 to 1838. Thomas Barge (d.1825) was also at Broughton Bridge and both were clients of Joseph Lockett for engraved rollers.

BRISSAC, PETER ABRAHAM DE   1731-68. Of Huguenot descent, he was related to several London silk weavers. One of his three daughters was presumably the Miss Brissac who married John Ware, calico-printer at Crayford, in 1778. De Brissac's account book from January 1760 to December 1762 provides much information on the work of this freelance designer for woven silks and printed cottons.

BROAD OAK, Accrington, Lancashire.   Printing began here in 1792 under the firm of Fort, Taylor and Bury, who also had printworks at Oakenshaw and Sabden. Taylor retired and Thomas Hargreaves joined the firm, taking it over in 1811 (when Fort and Bury concentrated their efforts on Oakenshaw and Sabden respectively) as Hargreaves and Dugdale. Thomas Hargreaves died in 1822, Dugdale in 1838, when the sons of Hargreaves carried on as Hargreaves Bros. & Co., still flourishing at the time of the article on the printworks in *The*

Journal of Design in 1850. Steam power was introduced at Broad Oak in 1813. From the 1820s the firm benefitted from the combination of finely engraved rollers by Potts and chemical advances made by their own chemist, Thomas Lightfoot.

BROMLEY HALL   One of the printworks on the banks of the River Lea in Middlesex, it was the first listed in the Excise books when duty was imposed in 1712. Benjamin Ollive was mentioned as a calico-printer in a document of 1720. The firm was known as Ollive & Talwin (1763-1783), Talwin & Foster (until 1790), Foster & Co. (until 1823).

BROWN, ROGERS & CO.   Linen-drapers at 157 Cheapside, London, from at least 1780 to 1810. The name of this firm is inscribed on a number of William Kilburn's surviving designs for printed cottons. Thomas Brown claimed to be the proprietor of one of Kilburn's designs in 1787; and Kilburn married the daughter of one Thomas Brown, described as an East India Director.

DUDDING   Oakley, Dudding & Co. were 'furniture printers' at 67 New Bond Street, London, from 1802 to at least 1805. By 1806 the firm had changed to Dudding and Nelson. Some of their cottons were printed at Bannister Hall; but they may also have had connections with Dudding, Chesson & Stevens, calico-printers at Beddington Corner, Surrey, around 1807-09. In 1810 Dudding and Nelson moved to 72 New Bond Street, where E. B. Dudding appears without partner in directories from 1811 to 1814. His stock was taken over shortly after that date by George Oakley. Upholders of that name operated in London from the late 18th century and may have been identical with Dudding's first partner.

DUGDALE   See Broad Oak. Also John Dugdale & Bros. wove cotton at Lower House, Padiham, near Manchester, from 1812; adding a small printworks in 1819 which was still operative in the 1840s.

EDWARDS, JOHN   Flower painter, active around 1763 to 1806. Exhibited mainly with the Society of Artists of which he was Director in 1776; but also at the Free Society (1763) and at the

Royal Academy (1786-88). In 1770 he published *The British Herbal* with one hundred colour plates.

FENN, CHARLES An artist specialising in birds and flowers, Fenn drew birds for engravings published by Robert Sayer in *The Ladies Amusement* and probably also for his *New Book of Birds*, published in 1765. These collections of motifs and vignettes were used as models by calico-printers and other manufacturers.

FIELDING & BROS. See Watson, Myers, Fielding & Co

FORDINGBRIDGE Calico-printing at Fordingbridge, Hampshire, was carried on by William Renger, bankrupt in 1778, and by John, Peter and Robert Reed, bankrupt in 1784. Peter Read continued printing until 1792.

GODDARD, DANIEL Known only from his surviving designs for calico-printers of the 19th century, Goddard's work was printed by Vint & Gilling of Crayford, Kent, and at Bannister Hall near Preston, Lancashire, for leading London linen-drapers such as Richard Ovey (1790-1831), Atkinson & Clarance (1781-1806) and Kinsey and Chambers (1801-21).

ILETT, JOSEPH O'Brien mentions a new purple of Ilett's put before the Society for the Encouragement of Arts some time before 1790. On 21st February 1809 he took out a patent (No. 3208) "for producing fast greens on cottons", the first true single green invented in Britain. Carl Wilhelm Scheele (1742-86) had produced a watery green made from arsenite of copper; and a better green called "vert faïence" based on peroxide of tin was discovered at Jouy in 1808.

JACKSON, JOHN BAPTIST He was born in or probably before 1700, being described as "in his old age" in 1755, and was dead by 1777. Jackson worked in Paris from 1725 to 1730 and in Italy from 1731 to 1754. In that year he published *An Essay on the Invention of Engraving and Printing in Chiaro Oscuro...* Some time after 1761 he went to Scotland, where he was employed designing printed cottons, and possibly also linen damasks and carpets, from 1765 to 1770. He was subsequently seen by Thomas Bewick in Newcastle "quite enfeebled with age", and died in an asylum on the Scottish border, protected by Sir Gilbert Elliot who died in 1777.

JONES, ROBERT Jones established a printworks at Old Ford, Middlesex, some time before April 11th 1757, when he advertised concerning a runaway apprentice. He signed and dated plate-printed cottons in 1761 and 1769, but the names of his artists did not appear. Three of them were given Society of Arts premiums in 1768 and 1772, but none of the designs of William Naylor, John Dew or John Philpot can be identified. Robert Jones sold out in 1780, when his stock of designs comprised "200 copper-plates and 2,000 Blocks and Prints".

KILBURN, WILLIAM 1745-1818. See Brown, Rogers & Co. Apprenticed at Lucan, Ireland, to the calico-printer Jonathan Sisson, Kilburn specialised in drawing and engraving. When freed from his apprenticeship, he went to London and worked freelance, participating in the *Flora Londinensis* of William Curtis. A calico-printer, Newton, offered him a partnership at Wallington, Surrey, and in seven years he bought out Newton. According to his own evidence given when seeking copyright protection for calico designs in 1787, he was one of six Master Printers around London who drew their own designs.

LIGHTFOOT, THOMAS See Broad Oak

LIVESEY, HARGREAVES, ANSTIE, SMITH & HALL Calico-printers of Manchester and Mosney, near Preston, built up a large business over about ten years, but overreached themselves and went bankrupt in 1788. They introduced machine-printing in 1785-86 and were threatened with arson by their workers.

LOCKETT, JOSEPH Engraver and cylinder-maker in Salford and Manchester, he was generally accepted to be the finest engraver of the early 19th century working for calico-printers. Dated strike-offs from his rollers, with details of the clients, survive from 1806 to 1840. His sons, Joseph Lockett and Bros ran a printworks near Manchester from 1828 to 1832.

LOWE, JOHN & CO., Shepley, Lancashire. Shepley Hall was established as a printworks in 1777 by Thomas Phillips and John Nash. They took John Lowe into partnership, and when they left to join other concerns, the firm became Lowe, Cottrell, Wood and Dalton in 1797. John Lowe took over the works alone in 1803 until his death about 1829, when the firm became Peter Brooke & Brothers.

MARSHALL, JOHN & SONS, Manchester.   This firm appears in the directories as calico-printers from 1818 to 1824.

MATLEY, SAMUEL & SON, Hodge, Cheshire.   Samuel Matley, calico-printer, was in partnership with James Lever at Red Bank, Manchester, until 1787, when Matley took over the business. Between 1802 and 1805 he was also printing at Scotland Bridge, Manchester, then letting those premises and moving to Hodge, near Mottram, where his family continued to print until 1870.

MAUDE   In 1802 William Maude married the daughter of James Greenaway of Livesey Fold, Darwen, a printworks twenty miles from Manchester. The brothers-in-law Potter & Maude went bankrupt in 1831.

MAXWELL, ROBERT   Calico-printer at Merton Abbey in Surrey, from some time before 1780, he went bankrupt in 1783. His copper-plates were acquired for printing at Bromely Hall. Impressions from forty of Maxwell's plates survive in the Musée de l'Impression sur Etoffes, Mulhouse.

MERCER, JOHN   Mercer was a weaver who turned to chemistry in 1818, when he invented an antimony orange. His greatest successes were with the application of manganese bronze and chrome yellow, and the mercerisation of cotton, to which he gave his name. Notes of his inventions, collected by his son for the Royal Society, are in a transcription by John Graham, made around 1846, preserved in the Manchester Public Library.

MILES & EDWARDS   Furniture-printers from 1821 to 1847. William Miles, linen-draper, was established from at least 1805 in Holborn, moving to Oxford Street in 1811. He had some cottons printed at Bannister Hall in 1806. Miles and Edwards, appearing first in the directory of 1822, probably set up their other Oxford Street address in April 1821, the date of the first sample in their order books T.209-T.211-1925. The firm's stock was taken over in the late 1840s by Charles Hindley who continued to produce their more popular patterns for several decades.

NIXON, FRANCIS   Died 1765. He introduced copper-plate printing from Drumcondra in Ireland to a printworks at Phippsbridge, near Merton, Surrey, established by George Amyand in 1752. Nixon and Amyand operated as partners there from about 1757 to the death of Nixon in 1765 and Amyand in 1766, the firm then being known as Nixon & Co until the printworks was sold in 1789.

O'BRIEN, CHARLES   Author of *The Callico Printers Assistant*, Volume I published in 1789, Volume II in 1792 under the title of *A Treatise on Callico Printing*, reprinted in 1795 under the title *The British Manufacturer's Companion and Callico Printers Assistant*. In 1789 he styled himself "Designer and Metallic Fancy-Figure worker for Cylindrical, Copper Plate Press, and Block Printing" and kept a drawing school and circulating library. In 1792 he advertised books sold by himself "(late Designer to Mr Kilburn) Pattern Drawer and Operator in Metal for Block or Cylindrical Printing, in Sets and Trails, to Callico-Printers in general". In 1795 he called himself 'Callico Printer'. He lived at Islington in this period.

OVEY, RICHARD   Active from 1790 to 1831. He styled himself 'Furniture Printer' but did no printing, being a linen-draper who commissioned designs and sent out work to the printworks of his choice. He used mainly the Bannister Hall works near Preston, but also printers in Carlisle and at Crayford, Kent. One of the leading London linen-drapers of the period, he supplied the Prince of Wales (later Regent) and other members of the Royal Family.

PEEL & CO.   The Peels, in various partnerships and at a number of different locations in Lancashire and Staffordshire, with wholesale firms as outlets in London, were the most successful of the Lancashire cotton manufacturing and printing families. They were at Church, near Accrington, from 1772 to 1840.

PEELE & SIMPSON   Wholesale linen-drapers in London "chiefly for Printed Goods and Muslins" (Mortimer, 1763). John Peele took out a patent in 1766 for "Printing images, songs, maps, landscapes and sea-pieces, by copper-plates, on linen for handkerchiefs". Some of the handkerchiefs commissioned by Peele and Simpson were engraved by D. Richards and printed by Rupert Davids, Crayford.

PROCTOR & BROWNLOW   leading London linen-drapers, 1792-1826, customers of the Bannister Hall printworks.

RAYMOND FRANCIS   This calico-printer at Lea Bridge in the 1790s could be the artist referred to as an 'Old Master' in 1833, and one of the six Master Printers round London who drew their own patterns in the 1780s.

RICHARDS, DAVID   See Peele & Simpson.

SWAISLAND, CHARLES   By 1809-10 Charles Swaisland was in business supplying holly wood-blocks to other printing firms. An article written in 1897 stated that his career began as a designer. As a printer, he employed many talented designers and purchased dsigns from Paris, protecting his copyright by registering large numbers of designs for dress materials and shawls. His firm was famous for block-printing fine woollens, flannels, plushes and, above all, shawls. Over 120 block-printers were employed in 1844, more than 500 hands in all in 1847. Swaisland Printing Company, after his death in 1865, continued until 1893.

TALWIN & FOSTER   See Bromley Hall.

THOMSON (THOMPSON), JAMES F. R. S.   Ran a large printworks at Primrose, Clitheroe, Lancashire, where he employed some 800 hands in 1833. Mainly concerned with block-printing, he took a great interest in new styles and designs, being, he said, one of about half a dozen manufacturers who then employed their own designers. Most of his designers had served an apprenticeship in the manufactory. He sometimes went to Paris in search of ideas for his designers, and in the 1820s had visited Mulhouse to assess the competition. In 1833 he gave this and other information in evidence before a Select Committee on Commerce and Manufactures.

VAUGHAN, THOMAS   Described as "pattern-drawer and print-cutter" in a London Directory of 1790, he established the firm of Thomas Vaughan & Sons, still active in 1835. The firm does not appear in directories of the later 1830s. A descendant of Thomas Vaughan sold several designs to the Museum (E.1819 to E.1841-1924).

WAGNER, JOHN   A calico-printer at Wallington, Surrey, bankrupted in 1803. He, or others of the same name, formed partnerships at Carshalton, Surrey, and Wimbledon which broke up in the 1780s. Another, or possibly the same Wagner, was printing calico at West Ham in 1796. Any or none of these could be Wagner the designer remembered as an 'Old Master' in 1833.

WARE, JOSEPH, MARY AND JOHN   Calico-printers at Crayford, Kent, Joseph and Mary each had their names on printed handkerchiefs of 1769 and thereabouts. An order book survives for 1773-75 with the name of Mary Ware. In 1781 she was in partnership with John, and they were bankrupt in 1782. John Ware married Miss Brissac in 1778.

WATSON, MYERS, FIELDING & CO   Were calico-printers at Catterall, Lancashire, by 1787, when four of their apprentices absconded. The partnership was dissolved in 1799, Henry, Benjamin, Joseph and Jeremiah Fielding taking over as Henry Fielding & Brothers. They ceased to print in 1830.

WILLEMENT, THOMAS   1786-1831. A writer on heraldry and an artist in stained glass, Willement also designed furnishings.